Fellowshipping with His Voice

Walking in God's Fullness Series

Dr. Pete Sulack

and Dr. Tony Slay

xulon PRESS

Table of Contents

Forward

M ost people hear the voice of God, however, because of lack of understanding or misconception, they find themselves ignoring or even resisting what they hear. They don't really know what to expect or what to look for. I always tell people if you are hearing voices out loud on a regular basis when you are by yourself, you probably need mental healing or to be set free from the oppression of the enemy.

All born again believers in Jesus Christ had to hear Gods' voice before they were saved, yet it seems that after their salvation experience, they act as though God quit talking when Jesus Christ rose from the dead. The Bible says that the Father must draw a man to be saved.

Coming to God through Jesus Christ in 1971 at the Oxford, Alabama football stadium was the beginning of a walk that most would not conceive possible and yet it would be eight years later that I would begin to hear and understand the voice of God on a regular basis. Yes, receiving the promise of the Father - Jesus' baptism that John preached about, the baptism of the Holy Spirit - I began to hear the voice of the Lord on a regular basis.

Going after knowing God has been my life's ambition. It has been a life of prayer, study of Gods' Word, and fellowship with other people - that have set themselves to seek God and His Kingdom – that has brought us into such a great understanding of the voice of God. With my wife, Elaine, and my twin daughters, Amy and Rachel, we have walked in blessed places, ministering to millions of people around the world because we know God's voice. We have known God's love. We have known God's peace. We have known the victory of the Lord Jesus Christ. We have experienced God's abundant life because we know God's voice. I would not trade my life experiences with anyone else in this world. God is good to me.

God has had me on a journey of Youth Evangelism, Youth Pastoring, Evangelism, Church Planting, Radio, TV, being a Christian School Principal, being in charge of Church Day Care Center, Church Bible College, Missionary Evangelism, Assistant Overseer of an International Fellowship of Ministers, Head of an International Ministerial Fellowship, President of a Bible College, and now the CEO of Ministry International Inc. and President of Ministry International Institute (MII). Ministry International Inc (MII) is a helps and resource ministry to ministers. Ministry International Institute is accredited education that is placed in the local church to help Pastors train up leaders and ministers.

This is how I met Dr. Pete Sulack. I met him at a friend's house and God told me about his call to mass evangelism. I shared this with him and yet God had not brought him to this place in ministry yet. It wasn't very long before God began to set Dr. Pete up for his future. I never dreamed that God would give me a chance to be a part of what Dr. Pete is called to do. However, as God opened the door to world evangelism for Dr. Pete, I received a call from him to come and minister to the Pastors in mass conferences. As a minister to ministers and all of the wonderful experience God has given me, it has been a ministry fit.

Working with a successful Doctor that is zealous for God is a great privilege. His hunger for the Word, and to know God, is unmatched among the many ministers I've known.

His passion to reach people with the goodness of God and the truth found in Jesus Christ is not to be compared. Just as our example, Jesus Christ - Dr. Pete is bringing healing to those that are hurting around the world. Through Matthew 10 Ministries International he supports totally hundreds of children with the following: place to stay, food, clothing, and education with Jesus Christ. At our crusades, and even sometimes up to thirty days before, he feeds and ministers to thousands of widows, supports and ministers to thousands of pastors, and preaches to the masses around the world.

Dr. Pete's great strength comes from the grace of fellowshipping God's voice. When he asked me to co-author a book that would bring people the simplicity of knowing God's voice and entering into that fellowship, I counted it a great joy and honor.

Be very careful. The truth that you will receive from reading this book will set you on a course to know your God and fulfill a life of purpose and blessing.

Dr. J. Tony Slay, CEO
Ministry International Inc.

Introduction

My desire is simply this: to share with you the privilege of being a child of God – to know God; to fellowship with God; to be in a personal, intimate relationship with God Himself. Is it awesome? Absolutely! Is it exciting? Without a doubt! Is it challenging? Most days! Is it worth it? More than anything in the whole world!

My feeling is this: if people only knew the privilege I have of being a child of God – the joy that's often unspeakable, the peace in the midst of a storm that is beyond understanding and the favor that at times seems to surround me as a shield – they would beg for the Jesus I know.

This is the premise I want to share with you. You can fellowship and *KNOW* God and as a result live a life beyond your comprehension. Whether you've never entered into a relationship with God, you've just started the journey, or you've been in church your whole life – this is a book for you. So buckle up and get ready, because your life will never be the same.

My friends, God can use you, but even greater than that, He wants to use you. A time frame doesn't qualify you. A degree or denomination doesn't set you apart. It simply comes down to your ability to *HEAR* God, because if you can hear Him (which you can!), then you can know Him, and if you know Him, He can use you in a significant and powerful way.

Dr. Pete Sulack
Matthew 10 International Ministries

Section 1

How to Hear God's Voice

Chapter One

God Is the Voice

Have you ever heard from God? Have you ever known something so strongly that you just couldn't ignore it? This is what happened to Peter in Matthew 16:13-17. Jesus asked His disciples, *"Who do men say that I, the Son of Man am?"* And they responded, *"Some say You are John the Baptist, some, Elijah; and others, Jeremiah, or one of the prophets."* So Jesus asks again. *"But who do you say that I am?"* Then in verse 16 Peter makes an amazing statement! *"Thou art the Christ, the Son of the Living God."* Jesus responded, *"Blessed are you, Simon Bar-Jonah, for flesh and blood has not revealed this to you, but My Father who is in Heaven."* Jesus was flesh and blood standing in front of them. Do you understand what Jesus said? In effect, He said, "Simon, I did not tell you this. You heard directly from My Father who is in Heaven." Jesus tells Peter that he is blessed. Why? Because he heard from the Father in Heaven. This is one of the great truths of the Bible. Anytime someone is blessed, the blessing comes from God Himself! So, when Jesus tells Peter he is blessed, He is letting him know that God has become involved in Peter's life. Jesus is saying, "You have heard from My Father who is in Heaven." How could this be? That Peter heard from the Father? We know there wasn't a loud voice. We know that it didn't thunder and lightning like it did with the children of Israel on Mount Sinai. Peter simply heard the still, small voice. It was so simple that Jesus had to tell Peter it was from the Father. We can hear from God, too. And if we hear from God, we can see His blessings in our lives.

God desires for all of us to experience the blessings of knowing Him. In order to walk in His blessings, you must have the confidence to know that you HEAR God. Even Jesus said in John 5:19, *"I tell you the truth; the Son can do nothing by Himself. He does only what He sees the Father doing. Whatever the Father does, the Son also does."* Why? Because hearing from the Father is the only way to walk in the fullness of God. To live life in any other way than by the Father's leading is a life of mere futility.

Even at the early age of five, I remember sitting on the bottom bunk in my bedroom. My mom had just received a call from a friend of hers saying that her little five-year-old daughter had just given her life to Jesus. Sitting there, the only thing I remember saying was, "I want Jesus in my heart." At the time, I don't even remember my mom talking to me about Jesus. Truthfully, there are not too many things, if any, that I remember from when I was five. But, even to this day, it is vivid in my mind, sitting on the edge of the bottom bunk next to my mom, and inviting Jesus to come into my life and be my Lord and Savior. That burning desire was placed within me to have what my little friend had – to have Jesus live inside me and to live for Him. I didn't know all about Jesus, but the Father was drawing a five-year-old child unto Himself. "I tell you the truth, unless you change and become like little children, you will never enter the Kingdom of Heaven."

Do you remember those high school years? All the changes. Trying to fit in. Finding yourself. Your identity. A perfect season for God to speak. If ever there was a time for the Father to speak, and speak often, it had to be high school. Take a minute to think back. It was a time during which the Father was speaking, often times likely to deaf ears. I can still remember a lot of the good and bad about high school, and the grace of God that gets us all through. It was a time that, while I might not have realized it then, God spoke quite often. That still small voice encouraging me to avoid certain crowds. That gentle nudge saying, "You are getting too close to that girl; slow down." That constant reminder from a teacher or parent to stay focused on school work because of the benefits this would later reap. Those early desires to make a lasting impact. The Holy Spirit's prompting for me to continue my education. That omnipresent voice that whispered, "press into God" when the distractions of this world kept pulling me from fellowshipping with Him. Or maybe that one thing missing, that no matter how great life seemed to be, I knew there was something more. I still vividly remember going to school everyday, knowing that many of my friends didn't know Jesus, and I could be that vessel God used to save them! I faced a constant struggle to live a life that reflected Jesus.

Does God speak all the time or just in the major points of our lives? Looking at my life, I can honestly say He has spoken in those pivotal parts, but Praise God, in those times that seem less significant, God's voice rings clearest. I say, "Lord, my bank account is in the red?" He says, "It is okay. Remember My Word." "God, the doctor says this." "Yes, but My Word says this." "God, everything seems to be falling apart!" "Yes, my child, but I have everything under control, rest in Me!"

God is a Spirit

God is a Spirit. The Bible tells us so in John 4:24: *"God is a Spirit, and those who worship Him must worship Him in Spirit and in truth."* God is a Spirit, and the way that the

Spirit can express Himself is in manifestation as spoken in 1
Kings 19:11-12:

> *"And He said, Go forth, and stand upon the mount*
> *before the LORD. And, behold, the LORD passed*
> *by, and a great and strong wind rent the mountains,*
> *and broke in pieces the rocks before the LORD;*
> *but the LORD was not in the wind: and after the*
> *wind an earthquake; but the LORD was not in the*
> *earthquake."*

I don't know about you, but if I am surrounded by a
group of people, or by myself, and all of the sudden there's a
wind, an earthquake and a fire, it's going to get my attention.
But, this passage says that God wasn't in those things. They
were present before He showed up. The wind, the fire, and
the earthquake were just an announcement. God is saying
"I'm about to show up, I'm about to move in your life, I'm
about to accomplish something in you." So the wind of God
blows. I have been at many revivals where everyone has left
talking about the wind, the fire, and the earthquake. All these
things are great, but if that is all people come away with,
then they missed what God was doing. It is about what is
right behind the wind, the earthquake, and the fire that God
wants to reveal to us. All the cool stuff is to get people's
attention in order to prepare them for what's next.

God Is the Voice

Then there is "the still small voice." You have to
understand that if you are a spirit, and you're dealing with
a natural world, then the way you manifest yourself to that
natural world is through your voice, and through what you
say. God desires to speak to us. The wind, the fire, and the
earthquake are introductions to prepare our hearts to hear
from God.

God's desire is to show us who He is by what He says. In the book of Exodus, the children of Israel were at Mount Sinai. Moses had brought them all there so that God could talk to them. The Bible talks about the darkness, the thunder and the lightning, and then all of the sudden, the voice of many words shows up. God from the beginning of time has desired a relationship with everyone. A personal relationship where He communicates with us Spirit to spirit. In Romans 8:16 Paul writes, *"The Spirit Himself bears witness with our spirit, that we are children of God."* How do we know we're hearing God's voice? It is that small voice inside, that according to James 3:17, *"is first pure, peaceable, gentle, easy to be entreated, full of mercy and good fruits, without partiality, without hypocrisy."* Anything contrary is something that is not from God.

When Jesus came to the earth, it was for God to reconcile the world to Himself through Jesus. Jesus is the Son of God, and came to the earth in the flesh, and walked as a vessel that contained God. He was saying, *"I only do what I see My Father do; I only say what I hear My Father say."* Jesus is saying, "When you see Me you've seen the Father." Jesus said in 1 John 4:12, *"No man has seen God at anytime, but if we love one another, then He dwells in us and His love is perfected in us."* God dwells in us. Jesus is saying, "I'm the tabernacle of the fullness of God; I'm the tabernacle for the Father and the Holy Spirit" And since He is the tabernacle of the Father and the Holy Spirit, He is able to say what God would say in a particular situation; He is able to do what God would do in the same situation. This is where those in relationship with God are supposed to be. We are supposed to come into an intimate fellowship with God where we hear His voice and do what He calls upon us to do.

In Genesis 3:8, we read about Adam and Eve dwelling in the Garden. It says they heard *"the voice of the Lord God walking through the garden."* God is the voice. In order to have a relationship with God, you will have to fellowship with the voice. Many say, "I would rather just read the Bible and save the talking to God part for later." When you read the Bible, consider that even though it is inspired by God it was written to all of us. It is great to read the Bible, but I need God to speak to me personally in a time of cell phones, iPods, and 21st century media. How does He desire to speak? First of all, He speaks through His Word – the Bible – as well as through our circumstances, our thoughts, and through other people.

There is only one way to have a relationship with God – through Jesus Christ; but there are many ways a person can come to Jesus Christ. He draws some to Himself one way, and He draws others another way. In the same way He speaks to some one way, and to others another way. God wants to have an intimate, personal relationship with each of us.

Chapter Two

Finding Your Purpose through His Voice

Daniel was thrown into the lions' den, and then he was saved from the jaws of lions. Shadrach, Meshach, and Abednego were thrown into the fiery furnace, and then they were saved from the flames. It is this personal walk with God and hearing God's voice that allowed Daniel to have the kind of peace that enabled him to be okay, even inside a lions' den. It was the fellowship Shadrach, Meshach, and Abednego shared with God that allowed them to know God's voice, and walk into a fiery furnace knowing God would be with them and protect them. There are many different scenarios I can share with you which are great testimonies of those who know the voice of God. I can read about Moses and what he was called to do. I can read about Joshua and what he was called to do. God has a calling for each of us as we learn to listen to His voice and walk in obedience to His call for us.

Recently, I held a redemption festival in a third world country. A few weeks prior to the trip, I got word that a militia group was making threats towards anyone that would preach the gospel there in the open air. All our plans were already in place. We had the grounds for the outdoor meeting paid for. We had all our preliminary work done: airline tickets purchased, hotels booked...and then we received word that we couldn't come. Let me tell you from firsthand experience, when your life and the lives placed under your authority are threatened you need to be able to hear from God in a personal and specific way. As I waited on the Lord and fellowshipped with Him, He showed me and gave me a supernatural peace that it was going to be okay for us to go. Praise God for the privilege of hearing His voice! What God did as a result was amazing! Instead of a three-day crusade, He told us to do a five-day crusade, and He showed up in a powerful way. I had the privilege of preaching the gospel to 350,000 plus people in person over the course of five nights – the largest crowds that city had ever seen. In just a few months following that festival, churches in the area grew by over one thousand members, and twelve new churches were planted. Lives were changed forever, because we were able to hear from God!

Without a personal relationship with God in which we can hear and discern His voice, it is impossible to enter into the plans and purposes God has destined for us. God is the One that will let me know what my purpose is and what I am called to do. I can read, I can quote, I can confess, and I can run around and say I want to do this and that. But I need to know the plan for my life. Otherwise, I'll end up working myself to death doing all of these things that God hasn't even called me to do. Without guidance, I would be left with a feeling of dissatisfaction in life. I must choose to come into a relationship with God and learn to hear His voice in order to find my purpose.

In my third year of chiropractic practice, the company experienced great success. One day as I pulled into our parking lot, I happened to glance up at our billboard, and God spoke to my spirit. He simply said, "Take away all your marketing for the next few months." It caught me off guard.

Truthfully, it offended me. "Lord," I remember thinking, "I honor You with my business, and our marketing has provided great visibility and a great return." He simply replied, "Trust Me" We must be able to hear and discern His voice. I was being called to do something that didn't make sense to me, so I decided to wait on God. Waiting is probably one of the hardest things in our lives that we are ever called upon to do. Personally, I would rather go-go-go! In Isaiah 64:4 it says: *"Eye has not seen nor ear heard of the things that God has reserved for those who wait upon Him."*

The word *wait* in Isaiah 64:4 is from the Hebrew word *chakah*, which means to look earnestly for and with great expectancy for what is to come. *Wait* is also used in Habakkuk chapter 2:3, and translates into *looking earnestly for that which is to come*. Waiting is contrary to what our flesh wants to do. My flesh wanted to move forward, but God told me to wait. Waiting on the Lord is a privilege. Isaiah describes waiting as a time in which God will speak to you, and reveal things in the Spirit. Waiting is for those who look earnestly for things to come, placing their eyes and hope in Christ; it is an expectation held for the God of this Universe to reveal His power and provision in a way that is beyond anything man could possibly imagine or understand. The power that the eye has not seen or ear heard is in store for those who wait on the Lord. How do we wait? Some position themselves to be alone with God, or they seek to calm all of life's distractions. In this instance, I simply stopped my marketing as God had suggested, and determined to wait until I heard from Him again.

While I waited I quickly became aware of the excellence of God's purposes. Within one week of putting an end to all of my marketing, a patient in my office mentioned that Mel Gibson was two months away from releasing the movie, *The Passion of the Christ*. Instantly, in my spirit I felt a burden for those who were lost. Over the next few weeks, God directed me to rent out four theaters and host the premiere of the movie. He instructed me in every detail for the food, the worship music, and the people who were to present the Gospel in each theater. To my surprise, the hype for the movie became so large that every major news station and media source in Knoxville was in attendance on the nights of the premiere. By the grace of God, I was able to share the Gospel on each news channel, radio station, and local paper as well as receive some national exposure. During the two nights that we premiered the film, we had close to one hundred people respond to the Gospel of Jesus Christ in a public theater. What had seemed an absurd thing to do – taking away all our marketing – resulted in more exposure and eternal fruit than I could ever have dreamed of. This was the product of God's desire for a personal walk with His child.

Hear and Obey

As a father of three boys, I find myself, frequently telling them to "listen and obey!" I am regularly informing them that life is so much easier when we just listen the first time and obey. In Deuteronomy 28:2, God spoke to Abraham and said: *"And all these blessings shall come upon you and overtake you, because you obey the voice of the LORD your God."* Once again in Genesis 26:5 God says: *"Because Abraham listened and obeyed My voice and kept My charges, commands, My statutes and My laws."*

I don't know anyone who doesn't want to have a blessed and prosperous life. God Himself wants us to be blessed. In Proverbs 10:22 we read, *"The blessing of the Lord makes one rich, and He adds no sorrow to it."* If God is not ashamed of His blessings being bestowed upon us, then we shouldn't be. But here is the key: "Abraham listened to the voice of God." If you are ever going to move forward with God, you have to listen. It is one thing to live off of someone else's blessing.

You can live off of generational blessings from family who have walked with God and loved Him. You can walk with people who have a generational blessing on them and receive some of the overflow. But God wants to bless your life and the plans He has for you, too.

I lived my whole life, up until four years ago, by what my earthly father said. My relationship with God was through my dad. I knew God by what my father said of Him. My reasoning was always that if he spent time with God, then I didn't need to figure it out on my own. Often, we let others dictate the plans for our lives rather than fellowshipping with God and listening to His voice and direction for our lives. It wasn't until I began to fellowship with God myself that I began to realize God had a plan and purpose for me that was different from the call placed on others around me. The more I am able to hear God and obey His voice, the more specific the call becomes in my life. Listening to others is great. Reading and hearing the stories of those who went before us is always helpful. But I need to hear God myself and know what I'm called upon to do.

Even more than hearing God concerning His purpose for our lives, we need to hear God through the day-to-day details of life. I have shared remarkable times with the Lord; times when He has begun to reveal His purpose and destiny for my life. Times when He has placed His desires in my heart, and they have burned within me. But not long after I have great encounters with the Lord, I find myself picking up the burden and yoke for what He has called upon me to do, and trying to make things happen on my own. I have found myself trying to figure everything out. It is during these times when we must hear from God, otherwise we will feel burdened by life. God says in His Word, *"My yoke is easy and My burden is light."* God wants us to walk in the freedom of fellowshipping with Him and hearing His voice. He wants to direct our paths! How great is it to know that

God wants to lead us and guide us to a life of victory? He can do this when we surrender our lives to Him and begin to know His voice.

A few years ago I had the privilege of publicly showing *The Passion of the Christ* again, this time to a group of homeless men, women, and children underneath a bridge in downtown Knoxville. I knew of an amazing ministry that had fed the homeless under this bridge for years and years. I had never been under this particular bridge, but had heard of the amazing work that had been going on there. A week prior to the big event, I held an all-night prayer service at my office to intercede for this event. I still remember it as though it were yesterday. In the early hours of the morning, we were left with only a handful of people. Three or four people laid hands on me to pray, and as they did, God brought me into a gravel parking lot. I could see Jesus setting up folding chairs, one after another. As I looked up, there was a huge bridge above me and all around the perimeter were these glorious figures like angels. In the distant parking lot, people were coming to sit in the chairs. Before they sat down, they were greeted by Jesus who said to each of them, "Come, for I have prepared a table before you in the presence of your enemies. Come and dine with Me." Each person was greeted one after another by Jesus the master servant! Then my attention was brought to a particular woman who seemed to be in rough shape, but nonetheless overjoyed to be sitting in one of the seats. I could see that she was blind in her right eye, and had to focus in order to see out of her left eye. Jesus turned to me and said, "If you will call this woman out after the altar call, I will heal her eyes." He then showed me another gentleman who was deaf. Once again Jesus said, "If you will call him out, I will heal him as well." Remember that I had never been underneath this bridge before, but in this vision, I knew it was the bridge we would be going to the very next week.

The night of the event came, and four or five hundred people were in attendance. Everyone was treated to live music, catered food, and a backpack filled with goods and necessities. When the movie finished, I got up and presented the Gospel. Afterwards, the Lord reminded me of what He had shown me the week before – the lady who was blind in her right eye, and the gentleman who was deaf. Friends, you have to understand, that I had never experienced anything like this before. This was completely new to me. By the grace of God, and with a lot of reservations, I mentioned to the crowd that the Lord had shown me these two people, and if this described anyone in the crowd please come forward. We waited for almost a full minute, which seemed like an eternity, and all of a sudden this lady from the back and man from the left side came forward. I watched with fascination because, before either of them reached the front the woman began to cry and then jump, and both of them shouted "I'm healed! I'm healed!" It was truly amazing. Before I knew it, God had shown me other people in the crowd with various illnesses. As God showed them to me I called them out. One gentleman in particular was so transformed by the experience that he came forward and emptied his pockets of his crack cocaine, placing it into the hands of the police officers.

My friends, if you can learn to hear God, and be obedient to His voice, you will see the glory of God move in ways you've never dreamed possible. In Exodus 15:26, God speaks:

"If you listen carefully to the voice of the LORD your God and do what is right in His eyes, if you pay attention to His commands and keep all His decrees, I will not bring on you any of the diseases I brought on the Egyptians, for I am the LORD, who heals you."

I have heard many people quote this Scripture. This is the first time God declares Himself a healer to humanity. But we must understand the context – to not only hear God's voice, but also to obey what He says to do. There are many paths one can take in various areas of life. When it comes to healing your body, there are multiple ways you can approach it. First, we must know God's perfect will. For it is impossible to overcome the storms in your life without knowing the perfect will of God. James talks about this in James 1:6-8:

"But when he asks, he must believe and not doubt, because he who doubts is like a wave of the sea, blown and tossed by the wind. That man should not think he will receive anything from the Lord; he is a double-minded man, unstable in all he does."

The Bible is clear about God's will for healing. There's quite a bit of Scripture on the subject. The Greek word *sozo* means salvation, deliverance, and healing. *"Whosoever shall call upon the name of the Lord shall be saved." "By His stripes we are healed." "By His stripes we were healed." "Lay hands on the sick, and they shall recover." "Is any sick among you? Let him call to the elders of the church; and let them pray over them, anointing him with oil in the name of the Lord. And the prayer of faith shall save the sick, and the Lord shall raise him up."* There were many people in the Bible Jesus walked by who were sick. But in every example where someone approached Jesus for healing, He healed them. Praise God, *"Jesus is the same yesterday, today, and forever."* These same miracles we read about in the Bible are the same miracles we can see today. And the same miracles we see all over the world in our redemption festivals, and in my office.

I hear so many people pray for healing by prefacing, "Lord, if it be your will...." Yet in Psalms 103, verses 2 and 3, David writes, *"Bless the Lord, oh my soul, and forget not all His benefits: who forgiveth all thine iniquities; who healeth all thine diseases..."* God heals all our iniquities (sins), and heals all our diseases. I have not heard anyone pray, "Lord if it be your will, forgive me," because we know "if we confess our sins, He is faithful and just to forgive us of all our sins and cleanse us from all unrighteousness." So why aren't people sure whether or not it is God's will to heal them?

Let's say, for example, that it isn't God's will for me to be healed. Then wouldn't going to the doctor, or taking medications, or having someone pray for my healing be disobedience? It is imperative that we know God's will on a subject. The Bible is filled with promise after promise concerning our relationship with God and the blessings we are entitled to as children of God. God's Word says that His promises (to us) are yes, and amen!

So, if we determine His perfect will on a subject, whether it is for healing, finances, or our relationships, we then need God to speak to us about how to approach the matter. Once we know it's God's will to be healed, the Lord will show us how to approach our healing. Even in Scripture, we see that He healed some one way and others another way. God desires to speak to us and lead us. God might want to heal some through the laying on of hands, others through corporate prayer, others through natural means, and still others through medical means. Whichever way He wants to work in us, we must learn to hear God's voice and be led by Him.

Fellowship Manifests Promises

I was speaking a few years ago and staying at a guest's home when a woman came to the door at five o'clock in the morning. We all woke up because she was pounding on the door. They came to get me and said there was someone who wanted to talk to me. I walked into the den, and she apologized saying, "I have to talk to you." She said, "I've had a plague for six months. It's horrible and the doctors can't do anything about it. Every morning I get up and read my Bible for an hour. And I still have this plague and I don't understand it." I said, "Tomorrow morning when you get up, instead of opening your Bible and just reading, talk to God for an hour. Talk to the God of the book. Say 'Here I am, I want to talk to you this hour,' and see what happens." Two days later she came running up to me grinning ear-to-ear saying, "I'm healed! I'm healed!"

You've got to get a hold of what I'm saying. I'm not telling people not to read the Bible. I just want to be honest with you. It is hard to grasp the truth of the Bible unless God uses the Holy Spirit to personalize it to my life. It's an instruction manual that doesn't work unless I can hear the author. I can continue to quote all the promises and blessings of God from now until Jesus comes back, but unless I'm walking with the God who authored the book, I'll live a cursed or sub-par life. We've got a lot of people meditating on the Word day and night, studying in order to feel accepted or validated. But they could be missing the relationship with the author of the book, and as a result lack the faith they require to operate what is in the book. God is saying, "I want you to come into the simplicity of this relationship that I have for you and fellowship with Me." We must learn to hear Him in order to know Him.

Chapter Three

How We Hear His Voice

And the very God of peace will sanctify you
wholly; and I pray God your whole spirit and soul
and body be preserved blameless unto the coming
of our Lord Jesus Christ.
1 Thessalonians 5:23

God created your spirit, soul, and body. I am a spirit, and in order to live here I have to have an earth suit. But inside this earth suit I am a spirit who has a soul, which is comprised of the mind, will, emotions, and intellect. In Ephesians 4:23 it says: *"Be renewed in the spirit of our mind."*

God is a Spirit and He created us as a spirit in His image so that He could communicate with us Spirit to spirit. When Adam and Eve failed to obey what God had relayed to them, they died spiritually; they were separated from God. When we give our lives to Jesus we are no longer separated from God, but reconciled to Him. The apostle Paul said "It is no longer I who lives, but Christ who lives in me." What does this mean? The Word of God says in 2 Corinthians 6:16:

"You are the temple of the living God."

This literally means that the walls have been torn down, and now God and I can fellowship together. God wants to fellowship with us so much that He says, "I'm just going to move in; I'm going to come live in you. You won't have to talk to me as though I'm way off somewhere else. We can talk Spirit to spirit through the person of the Holy Spirit." Jesus said "I'm sending a comforter to you." He talks about the Holy Spirit again in John chapter 16 and says, "The Holy Spirit will guide you in all truth" He will take what is God's and reveal it unto us. All things that the Father has are now ours. The Father and Jesus are able to minister to each of us through the Holy Spirit. Some people say, "I have never heard the voice of God." What you hear is Spirit to spirit, and all of the sudden you know something so strongly that it becomes alive in you, and it begins to have influence. You can't shake it. This is hearing God's voice. You aren't hearing random voices, but rather the voice of the Holy Spirit speaking into the spirit of your mind (your soul) with great influence. You can be assured it is God's voice you are hearing by getting your mind renewed in the Word of God. Paul tells us in Romans 12:2 *"Do not be conformed any longer to the pattern of this world, but be transformed by the renewing of your mind. Then you will be able to test and approve what God's will is – His good, pleasing, and perfect will."*

A few years ago, I was in India, shortly after the tragic Tsunami had hit Southeast Asia. I was sitting with a good friend when he got a call that his compassion organization had one hundred and five children they had found wandering the beaches on the east coast of India. All of these children had been left without shelter; food, and clothing, and ninety-nine of them had no remaining relatives of any kind. I can remember sitting there and this voice in my spirit said, "Take care of these children." I said, "What? Not me Lord." But, I couldn't shake this feeling that I was supposed to step up to this need. Day after day, I found myself thinking about those children. No matter what I found myself doing, the children wandering the beaches never left my mind. It was a voice with great influence that I could not shake. It was the voice of God. Now, a few years later, we are in the process of moving all one hundred and five children from a leased building to a brand new facility. All the children are living together under one roof, all in school, and all know and love Jesus!

The Problem

Let's talk about God in our lives – God's voice in our lives. The Spirit that manifests as a voice of many words will impact my life. In Genesis chapter 1, God creates the heavens and the earth. The Bible says that the Spirit of God moved on the face of the deep. Have you ever felt the Spirit of God move in you? How does it feel? Have you ever been in a service where you had a sickness, something was wrong with you, and then the Spirit of God moved all over you? But when you walked out you were still sick, still hurting or oppressed? How can I have problems after God has moved in me? That's the million dollar question, isn't it? The Spirit of God is in you and is upon all people. The Spirit of God is moving on the whole earth, and the whole body of Christ is filled with the Spirit of God, but for most of them there is no power or change in their life. What is the problem?

I want you to pay close attention to this. The Spirit of God moved on the face of the deep but NOTHING HAPPENED (in the natural) until God spoke. It is not that nothing was happening prior to God speaking, but it was as if the Holy Spirit was "brooding" over the planet, preparing it for what the Father was about to speak. In the same way a mother hen broods over her eggs to prepare them for hatching. Likewise, it is only because the Spirit is moving both on and in us that we can truly be prepared for what the Father is saying to us. Even though we are filled with the Holy Spirit, NOTHING can happen until we fellowship with God and know what He is saying.

God has given to every man a measure of faith. God tells us in the Bible that there is enough grace for everyone to be saved and begin a relationship with Him. The Bible also lets us know that the whole earth is filled with His glory. His glory is already here.

The apostle Paul states in Ephesians 1:3: *"Blessed be the God and Father of our Lord Jesus Christ, who has blessed us with every spiritual blessing in Christ."*

All blessings have been poured out, but it is imperative for us to know what God is saying to us. God is a Spirit, and the only way He talks and manifests His character is through what He says. Surely someone must have heard Him in the last 2000 years, or we're in big trouble. Did God really quit talking to us after Jesus rose from the dead and went to sit at the right hand of the Father in Heaven? Would He move into man as His new home and quit talking? If one person has heard Him, then all of us are able hear Him. If all of us are able to hear His voice, then all of us can come into a relationship with Him. How awesome is that?!

Some have said, "I don't need God to speak to me personally; I've got a whole book on what He has said." Again, the Bible is the Word of God, but until it is made alive by the Holy Spirit's personalizing, it's only words on a page. The Bible is applicable for all time, but must be made alive by God to each of us today. I need to know what God tells me to do specifically. In Mark chapter 4, there was a storm, and the wind came, and the disciples shook Jesus, crying out, "Jesus we are dying; don't you even care?" Then Jesus rebuked the wind and the sea and said, *"Peace be still."* It was a perfect depiction of Jesus operating out of His relationship with His Father. Jesus was saying and doing what His Father told Him to say and do and His desire is for us to do the same, by the power of the Holy Spirit, speaking through us.

Chapter Four

Releasing the Power of His Voice

The Scriptures John 5:19, John 5:30, and John 8:38 all illustrate how Jesus is working out of His relationship with His Father, and the way in which He only did what He saw His Father do. He only said what He heard His Father say. Jesus said *"It is written"* when He was in the wilderness. But you may remember that after He walked out of the wilderness, the angels came and ministered to Him. Another time the devils cried, "We know who You are. Have you come to torment us?" Why? Because God was with Jesus. You see, when Jesus was baptized in the Holy Spirit, the Father spoke from Heaven and said, *"This is my beloved Son with whom I am well pleased."* When Jesus graduated to the wilderness, the Father made His abode (residence) with Jesus. The fullness of God was manifested on the earth through Jesus Christ, and then Jesus did what He saw His Father doing; Jesus said what He heard His Father say. He was operating out of relationship. Look back at Mark 4 again, Jesus is asleep on the boat as it fills with water, and they the disciples have to wake Him up. How did He sleep during the huge storm? He slept in peace and when He woke up, He operated out of that peace. Jesus speaks, and instantly the wind and the sea obey. Was the Holy Spirit there already? When Jesus was asleep, we know that He was filled with the Holy Spirit, but nothing was happening. Someone had to say something. Someone had to speak something.

The principle of releasing the power of God's voice has never been so real to me as when I was invited to be a part of a worship service at the area rescue mission. This night was my first time attending, and I was asked to come and minister in healing. I had been told that these services were not structured, but completely led by the Spirit of God. I arrived that evening over an hour early, so I turned on some worship music in my car and waited on the Lord. I was hoping that God would give me some words of knowledge for people who God wanted to heal in the service. As I waited on the Lord, I struggled to receive anything...except one word – River. "River, Lord, what's that?" I remember wondering to myself, "What am I supposed to do with *River*? Can't you give me something more like cancer or deafness?"

The service started, and I took a seat in the front row and began to worship God. Roughly fifteen minutes into the service the gentleman leading worship stopped singing, and told the crowd of two or three hundred homeless, the majority of whom were asleep, that God was going to move in a big way. "Yeah right," I thought to myself, as I looked around at the sleeping crowd. Then God gently spoke to me, "Do you remember the river?" "What river?" I said. "You never gave me anything more." And then God began to speak to my spirit; not audibly, but in such a way that it got my attention. He said, "There is a river that is flowing from the stained glass cross behind the stage down the center aisle and back to the door. If you will tell everyone to get in the aisle, I will touch the people." "Who me?" I remember saying. "Are you crazy? This is my first time here." I went on. "They'll never let me back!" But it wasn't a river that I could see with my natural eyes. God was speaking to my spirit, that there was a river flowing in the Spirit down the center aisle and people needed to get in it.

Boy was it a battle. I mean it was my first time visiting the shelter, and this was completely outside the little box I had created for the way in which I believed God would move. Cautiously, I ventured out into the center aisle to see if I could feel anything. Nope! Then, trying not to attract attention to myself, I walked around to the other side of the chapel. When I got to the back, I felt the Lord say with almost deafening clarity, "If you don't speak out what I am telling you the river will be gone!" Instantly, I made my way back to the front and approached the head worshipper to share what I felt the Lord telling me. Without hesitation he gave me the microphone and I found myself telling the crowd of sleeping, homeless people, "God said there is a river flowing from the base of this cross behind me, down this center aisle and if you will get in it, you will be set free."

Before I could set down the microphone, there were people jumping into the center aisle as if a bomb had exploded inside of them. Within seconds there were more then seventy-five people in the aisle. I approached each of them and asked them what had happened. All anyone could say was, "I want Jesus!" That remarkable evening over fifty people gave their lives to Jesus, and many more were miraculously healed by the power of God.

That following week I returned to the shelter to give people chiropractic adjustments. A boy in his late teens was on the table. He told me that he had been at that service a few days before. He had just arrived from New York, and had grown up in gangs and had seen his mother and father both killed just a few months earlier. The evening of the *River* service he had wanted to give up on life. He shared that when the Lord said to get into the river, he began to weep uncontrollably. He now knew that God was trying to save him both physically and spiritually. He gave his life to Jesus.

God has given us the power to hear His voice, and if we are obedient to speak out what He tells us, He will release His power through us...the power that transforms lives!

Judging by the Word of the Father

Now I would like to show you how thoroughly Jesus was led by what the Father said. Jesus said in John 5:30: *"I can of mine own self do nothing. As I hear, I judge; and my judgment is just, because I seek not mine own will, but the will of the Father who sent me."*

Jesus said He judged everything with just judgment because He judged based on the will of God. He only judged what He heard His Father judge. But Christians today judge each other by what is written in the Bible. We look in the Bible, the written Word of God, and we read what the Lord says is right and what is wrong, and we judge one another on that basis. But Jesus did not come to condemn the world; He came that the world might have life! What a contrast! The only judgment that Jesus made was in reference to what the Father had judged. This is why His judgment is always just. For Jesus to make a judgment, He had to have heard it from the Father. Are we not supposed to be like Jesus? What will take the divisions and the schisms out of the body of Christ? It will happen when we learn to walk like Jesus.

Agree And Speak

"For verily I say unto you, That whosoever shall say unto this mountain, Be thou removed, and be thou cast into the sea; and shall not doubt in his heart, but shall believe that those things which he saith shall come to pass; he shall have whatsoever he saith. Therefore I say unto you,

what things soever ye desire, when ye pray, believe that ye receive them, and ye shall have them." Mark 11:23-24

In the above passage, Jesus is with His disciples, they had just passed by a fig tree, but the tree didn't have figs on it. For some reason, Jesus decides to curse the tree. Why? *"I only do what I see My Father do."* He did this because no man could eat the fruit from that tree. God speaks, it happens! You see, that's what the prophetic voice does on the earth. That's what God's voice in the church is supposed to be doing. When God speaks to you, you are supposed to speak what He is saying. You're supposed to bring forth what He is saying. You may not understand it but that is okay. Faith is the substance of things hoped for and the evidence of things not yet seen. In other words, whatever He is saying to you is something that needs to be brought from the Spirit to the natural. It's not something that's already in the natural. People always ask, "How can I be sure it was God and not myself?" You can by familiarizing yourself with the Word of God, the Bible, and godly people (I Thessolonians 5:19-22). Paul also writes in 2 Timothy 3:16, *"All Scripture is God-breathed and is profitable for teaching, rebuking, correcting, and training in righteousness."* So when you are able to confirm what God is speaking to you through confirmation in the Word and suddenly agree with what He is saying and doing, you must speak out and do what He shows you. How do I know to do this? We have the whole Bible full of men saying and doing what God told them to say and do. Thank God for His Word to show us examples. He said to Abraham, *"You will be the Father of many nations."* How do we know that God said that? Because Abraham told us what God said! How are people going to know what God has told you? You have to speak it. This is where we tend to mess up. We question and reason with our carnal mind. We must receive from God, believe against our environment, be familiarized with the inspired Word of God and say and do what He says.

All over the world, in our redemption festivals, as I preach the Gospel, God begins to speak to me. All of the sudden in the middle of the preaching, God will inform me that He wants to heal someone, and to speak it out. How does God inform me? He does it through a still small voice. It's a voice that I can't shake in the middle of my preaching. There have been numerous times when He has told me that He wants to heal someone with blindness, deafness, paralysis, or cancer. Early on in the ministry I would hear God speak these things, but I wouldn't speak it out. As I have learned to speak out what God is telling me, amazing miracles take place in the crowd. We have had testimony after testimony of people coming forward who were healed of major ailments. These individuals tell the crowd that Jesus touched them when I spoke their disease out. The more we can be in tune to what God is saying by familiarizing ourselves with God's perfect will in the Word of God, the more specific we can be in speaking it out and seeing the hand of God.

Have God's Faith

This entire chapter is about praying. It's about hearing God and releasing what He is saying. It's about operating out of a relationship with God. Jesus told His disciples as He looked at the fig tree in Mark 11, *"No man eats fruit of thee."* Spoken in our terms, the tree is dead! Peter heard it. The other disciples heard it. So the next day, they came by the tree and saw it was withered from the roots. Jesus tells Peter to have faith in God – have the faith OF God. You can read the Word at a faith level, but when God speaks to you, it is His faith you use and His faith is powerful! Everything – the fullness of God, the power of the Holy Spirit, everything will honor His faith. We should have the faith of God. Have you ever spoken to the mountains, and the mountains haven't disappeared? Why? You can't confess a mountain away. It isn't about your will; it's about God's will. Have faith in God. If God tells you to speak to the mountain, it will move. It will get out of the way. Speak to the fig tree, and it will wither, etc.

Desire. This is a really important word because it's tied to other Scriptures. God says He will put His desire into your heart if you will delight yourself in Him. He doesn't mean your carnal desires. He's not saying, "I'll give you unholy desires outside the Word of God." He's referring to your relationship with Him and your heart's desire transforming into His desire. When you have a personal relationship with God, He will put His desire into your heart. You can discern whether or not it's God's desire for you by asking whether or not you are delighting yourself in the Lord and, if so, does your delight line up with God's Word? The prophet Isaiah, in Isaiah 8:19-20 warns us, *"When men tell you to consult mediums and spiritists, who whisper and mutter, should not a people seek their God? Should they seek the dead on behalf of the living? To the law and to the testimony! If they do not speak according to this Word, it is because there is no light in them."* You have to ask, is this voice that I am hearing lining up with the Word of God? Years ago, a good friend of mine from graduate school decided that he could hear from God without ever spending time reading the Bible. When he would describe to me what he thought God was saying, it was completely contrary to God's Word. In a short period of time, these voices that he was hearing had caused my good friend to lose everything – his career, family, and way of life. This is a reminder to me that when God speaks, it will always line up with God's written Word – the Bible.

Believe that you will receive what you desire when you pray. Don't just speak something. Believe it! It's more than that. I've heard people say, "God will help if He wants to." But if that's the case, then prayer is irrelevant. The Bible doesn't tell me to go that route. The Bible tells me to stand on the Word of God and believe the Word. It also calls me into a relationship with the author of the Word so that what He is saying will come to pass. That's what we need. There are many people who are moving in healing, and this is because God told them to go into healing ministries. They heard God's voice and were confident in what He said, and were obedient to Him; this is why their ministries are seeing healings. You must be a doer of the Word, not just a hearer. You can raise the dead if He speaks to you. God is sovereign. God is not limited by us. He is bringing us into relationship with Him so that things begin to move around us, and the world begins to change around us, and we can be a part of it!

Section 2

When God Speaks

Chapter Five

When God Speaks, Faith Comes

In Romans 10:17, the apostle Paul writes: *"So, then faith cometh by hearing, and hearing by the Word of God."* The way this Scripture has been preached, the way it has been taught, and the way we have read it, is that faith comes by hearing, and hearing through the written Word of God. In other words, faith comes by meditating on the letter God gave us – the Bible. The more and more we read and hear the written Word, the more we will have faith. But in this particular Scripture we read, "Faith cometh by hearing, and hearing by the Word of God." The Scripture is actually not referring to the written Word, but rather to God's spoken Word. So this verse means that when we hear God speak, faith comes.

A Walk with God

Is it wrong to meditate on the written Word? No, absolutely not. It is actually commanded. Everyday, I spend time reading the Bible. We preach and teach out of the Bible. We find our examples there. We learn about what God has done for others. We understand what God will do. But still, we are not Daniel. We are not Shadrach, Meshach, or Abednego. We are not Peter. We are not Paul or Silas. You are you, and I am me, therefore, we need God to move for us. We need to see what God will do through us and for us. He might deliver us before we get thrown in jail. He might deliver us before we get thrown into a fiery furnace, or He could leave us there. This is our *personal* walk with Him. We need our own specific and individual instructions from God!

We can read the Bible and see what God has done with others and know that He is God, but when it comes to *our* lives, we need faith. The Bible says that the just will walk by faith. The Word of God says that faith comes by hearing and hearing through the spoken Word of God. In other words, faith comes from the spoken Word of the Father to you. You need your own personal walk with God! You can have it by hearing the Voice of God and fellowshipping with Him!

God's Voice Is Necessary

When we begin to hear the Father's voice, faith comes. Have you ever heard God say, "I love you"? Have you ever heard Him personally speak into your heart something like that? It could be the simplest thing and may inspire you to get out and run around saying, "Oh! God said He loves me! God said He loves me!" You'd be excited because you'd heard from the Father, and you'd believed what He said, which is faith. Some sing the song "Jesus loves me, this I know," but it does not thrill them at all. They may be happy that you are happy, but they may not understand your joy. Most of us know He loves us but, having heard the Father's voice, you'd have an in-depth insight that they do not have. Others know Jesus loves them because the Bible tells them so. But you'd know Him through having heard His voice! We need a Church that is in fellowship with God through hearing from God, and through the study of the written Word. Let's also look at John 10:2-3: *"But He that entereth in by the door is the Shepherd of the sheep. To Him the Porter openeth; and the sheep hear His Voice: and He calleth His own sheep by name, and leadeth them out."*

"To Him, the porter openeth." The 'Him' refers to Jesus, and the "porter" refers to the Father. This Scripture was based on hearing from God. All of Scripture is based on hearing from God. "His sheep hear His voice." Someone may say, "Well, I never hear the voice of God." If I had never heard the voice of God, then this Scripture alone would be enough to bring me to my knees because **Jesus said that His sheep hear His voice.** His sheep are His children – those of us who have a personal relationship with Him. In order to hear the Voice of God, we must be able to recognize it through our relationship with Him. For example, when I am in a crowded place with my family and my kids get away from me, it is easy for me to call out their name and they hear me. Why? Because they recognize my voice. When someone else calls their name they do not respond because they do not recognize the voice. It is the same with God speaking to us. God calls His own sheep by name. When He talks to me, He calls me "Pete." When He talks to you, He will call you by your name, too. You should expect it. If you haven't heard Him yet, be encouraged: the Word of God says that His sheep know His voice, and He calls them by name. I want that! After all, this is a personal relationship. I call Him by name, and He calls me by name.

Notice the Bible not only says that His sheep hear His voice, and He calls His own sheep by name, but He also leads them out. What is so wonderful about this Scripture saying *"and He leadeth them out"?* **What does God lead us out of? He leads us out of sin! He leads us out of darkness! He leads us out of cursing and into blessing! He leads us out of captivity! You could say He leads us out of the wilderness!** Unfortunately, some people love the wilderness. They live there. They have been there so long that they begin to enjoy it and believe that it is all there is. But God will lead us out of the wilderness and into the land of milk and honey. You will come out of that place of wondering where God is, into a powerful relationship Him. As you walk with the Father, His blessings will overtake you. It will happen when He speaks to you. Let me ask you, did He say you were going to be led out by a preacher? Did He say you were going to be led out by a Sunday school teacher? No, you are led out and delivered by hearing God's spoken Word to you!

Chapter Six

Salvation through God's Voice

The Word of God declares that God uses the "foolishness" of preaching the Gospel to save the lost. Paul calls it foolishness because all that a preacher can testify to is what God has done for them and what God has shown them. It's important to remember that your walk with God is different from anyone else's. So, how do you hear your own Word from God? Matthew 6:33 says: *"But seek ye first the Kingdom of God and His righteousness; and all these things shall be added unto you."*

As you begin to seek God earnestly, He will begin to speak and reveal Himself to you and His direction for your life. It is out of this relationship with God and seeking His face that you begin to recognize His voice. I have a brother-in-law who is a banker. He told me that bank tellers are told to become very familiar with authentic money. Why? So that they may learn to properly decipher the difference between counterfeit money and the real thing! God's desire for us is that we become so familiar with His voice through fellowshipping with Him, reading His Word, and spending time with Him, that we will learn to be sure it is His voice we are hearing.

51

Remember King Samuel as a young boy? God spoke to him in his bed over and over again, but Samuel assumed it was Eli. Why? Because He was unfamiliar with God's voice. My testimony may be similar to someone else's, such as David, John, Paul, or Abraham. You can read how God walked with them and moved in them; you might then hear my testimony and be inspired to have a testimony of your own, and to move toward God. This is why we share. Preaching calls us to move toward God, but when someone is saved in a service, it is not because of the preacher. Again, the preacher is sharing his revelation of God with others, but the hearer may not have heard what the preacher is sharing personally from the Father.

What causes a person to want to be saved? Jesus said that unless the Father draws someone to Himself, then the person cannot be saved. Jesus also said, "Him that cometh to Me, I will in no way turn away." Therefore, the man who hears a message will begin to hear God talking to him. God says, "This is your day to be saved; I will accept you; I will receive you." He may hold on to the back of the pew, his knuckles turning white with conviction because he knows he can be saved; he has heard from the Father. God is pulling this man to Himself.

One of the most amazing things I've ever witnessed is the Spirit moving on a crowd as I preach the Gospel. The message I preach is the Gospel in its simplicity: "God created a perfect world, sin destroyed it, Jesus fixed it, and you can receive it." As I preach the Word, it comes alive for people. Many times before I even do an altar call, people are running to the front to give their lives to Jesus. Why? Because as Paul describes in Romans 1:16: "...*The Gospel is the power of God to those who believe it.*" When the Gospel is preached, God begins to bring revelation to the people, making it alive, and the power of God is released. Even more than this, God begins to bring the people the revelation that

He is their source for everything – healing included. Before I even pray for the sick, people start getting healed of blind eyes, deaf ears, cancer, paralysis, and everything else you can possibly think of.

The praise and worship and preaching of the Word creates an environment for people in which they are able to hear from God. This is why we need to fellowship with other people who love God and fellowship with Him. We hear their testimonies inspiring us to go after everything God has for us.

Have you ever tried to minister to someone, but felt as though you weren't able to reach them? Even if you tell them all you've learned, you cannot do God's job for Him. This is, again, where faith comes into play, and a person has to receive his own revelation from God in order to heal.

I dined at the supper table with the King, but you are getting leftovers right now, even as you read. You are getting *what God has said* rather than what He wants to say to you now. The word I speak of brings life to me – it makes me excited! It will be life to you when you receive it from the Father. The revelation you get from the Father will lead you out of your struggles and give new direction to your life.

Chapter Seven

Revelation from the Father's Voice

If I get up and see you in the morning, eat breakfast with you, go through the day with you, and watch you operate all day, I will see you behave like a human, like a flesh creature, all day. We are all flesh creatures running around. It's only as Spirit-filled Christians with God's anointing that we have power in our lives. Exciting things are happening. People are being healed. People are being delivered. Even in the Old Testament, when Moses came bringing plagues by the power of God upon Egypt, the sorcerers and those who were in witchcraft duplicated most of the plagues that God used. It is nothing new to see power demonstrated.

Various people have lived in different ages saying that they were the Christ or the Messiah. But they have died, and their followers have fallen by the wayside. This is what some people thought would happen with Jesus. But Peter had a revelation about who Jesus really is in Matthew 16:16. He said, *"You are Christ, the Son of the Living God."* We do not know what things he might have seen Jesus do. He might have snored one night. We do not know. Jesus was flesh and blood, a person who Peter ate with. Peter walked with his

Lord on the earth for nearly three years, and yet he came out with this revelation. He said it out loud. Do you know how scary it would have been for Peter to say things that could have been considered blasphemous? Peter's pronouncement would have been justification for stoning. Anyone who had not had the same revelation as Peter would have thought they ought to have killed Peter for saying this.

How could Jesus be the Son of God? He was born in a manger. Some people even thought He was an illegitimate child. He was a carpenter before He started teaching. These are the facts. The Man ate and slept just like we do. Yet, when He stood up to speak, there was power in His words, and thousands listened to Him. They saw proof in His miracles and healings. Could they truly understand His words? Maybe. Maybe not. But in this instance, Peter was able to understand Jesus' question in Matthew 16 verse 13, and answer because he heard from God.

Chapter Eight

A Hearing Church

This is exactly what the church needs. We need to hear from our Father in Heaven. But the church may sometimes say things heard from flesh and blood only. We need to combine these words with a revelation from God, and shout it from the steeple tops. In Matthew 16:18, Jesus said: *"I say also unto thee, that thou art Peter, and upon this rock I will build My church; and the gates of hell cannot prevail against it"*

Upon what rock? It was upon the rock of hearing from His Heavenly Father, the revelation that Jesus was the Christ. It was upon hearing *a spoken Word* from Heaven – a living Word from Heaven! Jesus is explaining to Peter, when we hear from the Father that "It is a rock that the gates of hell cannot prevail against." Jesus is telling His disciples and teaching us at the same time that when God speaks it is an absolute truth! You can count on it! For instance, we know that gravity is an absolute truth, whether I believe in gravity or not, when I drop my keys they fall, because gravity is an absolute truth. In the same way Jesus is saying that when you hear from God, Spirit to spirit, you can count on it. But more than this– all hell cannot come against it. And this is the way God is going to build up and strengthen His people who are in relationships with Him – by speaking to them Spirit to spirit. Can you imagine what it would mean to you in a time of financial difficulty if God personally told you that He was turning your situation around? Can you imagine if your marriage was in trouble and God told you that He was going to restore it?

It is great for me to read the truth in the Bible, or for someone I know to encourage me, but it is quite different when God speaks personally to me. When God speaks to you, it is a rock that you can act on, trust in, and believe in. When you are confident in what God has said to you, you will see Him work and move in your life in such a way that all hell cannot prevail against it.

Through hearing the voice of the Father, Jesus explains in verse 19 of Matthew 16 that we will receive keys to the Kingdom of God. Since this Kingdom is inside the believer, we find that the fullness of God is in that Kingdom. Through Jesus Christ we have access to the keys that unlock our ability to fellowship with God. Matthew 6:10 says, *"Your Kingdom come, your will be done, on earth as it is in Heaven."* This is the revelation of how God releases His authority in you. Jesus is saying, "I give you the keys to the Kingdom of Heaven, and whatever you bind on earth will be bound in Heaven, and whatsoever you loose on earth will be loosed in Heaven."

Jesus is saying that through salvation, God has given us access to the Kingdom of God, and whatever God tells us to do, we can do it. Yes, by hearing His voice and perfect will, He releases us and gives us the authority to carry out His will. Jesus tells us that if we have heard from God concerning a certain matter, we have the authority to carry out what He has spoken. For instance, when God called me to the nations of the earth, He gave me authority to loose the finances to accomplish His vision. At the same time, He gave me the authority to bind and render powerless any opposition to what God has spoken for me to do.

Adam and Eve were kicked out of the Garden of Eden and out of God's presence because they disobeyed Him. But Jesus came to restore us to God so that we could commune and have fellowship with Him! John 14:6 says: *"I am the way, the truth and the life. No man cometh unto the Father but by Me."*

When you have been born again by surrendering your life to Jesus Christ, you can fellowship with the Father. The Father is the one who spoke to Peter. The Father will speak to you. Jesus said He would build His church by having His Father speak to us. Did you know that God's children are referred to as the bride of Christ? In a wedding ceremony, who gives the bride away? Her Father does. When he presents the bride to be married, the father ought to have done everything in his power to have prepared his daughter for life. Did you know that our Father is preparing us for His Son? In essence Jesus is saying in Matthew 16:18, *"Peter, I am going to build My church by having My Father talk to people. My Father will talk to those who have given their lives to Me. My Father will talk to My bride."* It is wonderful that we are the bride of Christ. It is wonderful that the Father desires to speak to us. *"Upon this Rock I will build My church and the gates of hell will not prevail against it."* When you have heard from the Father, all hell can come against you, but you will not lose your rock!

God's Rocks – My Rocks

When David fought Goliath, he did not fight with natural rocks, even though he had several smooth stones. He said, *"I was with God when the bear came. I was with God when the lion came. Who is this Philistine that he should defy the armies of the living God?"* Do you understand how David could speak so bravely to the giant? He spoke with the courage God gave him when he faced the bear and the lion. When David stood in front of the giant, he ran toward his foe with confidence. When we have a rock from God, it will not fail!

I love the gift of prophecy. Prophecies are from God. When a man prophesies by the Spirit of God to you, an anointed Word goes into your spirit. It is a divine impartation. It is not man speaking; it is God using man's voice. God speaks outwardly to you and into your spirit to confirm what He has already begun speaking to you. One way that God will confirm the prophecy you receive is through the counsel of others. When you do that, the gates of hell will not prevail against it.

As I now minister these words to you, I am throwing my rocks to you. God has given me a pocketful of rocks. He has spoken a lot of things to me, and I have understood a lot of things. They are the rocks God gave to me. You can take them and say, "Oh yes, I like these rocks." But in order for you to use them, God has to bring revelation to you concerning them. Without the revelation from God, you cannot use them effectively. When the word becomes a rock from God, you can now use it to minister to others, too. The only rocks which will work for you are the rocks that you personally receive from God.

I have a good slingshot with some solid rocks. God also wants to fill your pockets full of rocks! For what do we need rocks? We need rocks concerning our marriage: I want my marriage to be strong, so I need to hear from God about it. I want my children to grow up well and be saved. I need God's rocks for my children. I know that the Bible says that when I am saved and walk with God, my whole family will be saved.

I see the promise for my family in the Bible and it gives me hope. But it is not the *letter alone* that Jesus is building His church upon. He is building it upon hearing from the

Father. So, I not only look in the Bible, I also pray for a rock for my children. I want to know that my whole household will be part of God's family. I want to hear from God. Then I will have a rock that the gates of hell cannot prevail against!

I also need a rock concerning health, finances, and everything else. I need the Father to speak to me continuously. The more He speaks into my life, the more rocks I will have. I want rocks to throw to you. If you are sick, I want to throw a healing rock to you. If you are bound, I want to throw a deliverance rock to you. I do not want to just be saved, healed, delivered, and set free myself. I do not want to just be blessed. I want to be a blessing. I want to help those around me. I need to hear from Heaven.

How do you see the gifts of the Spirit at work? You need God to speak to you. You can count on what He says. Jesus is building His church on a rock and His sheep hear His voice. How does He lead us out? He gives us rocks! Every rock we have is a step into victory. He delivers us from darkness and gives us power to be over comers in this life.

Lights On, Darkness Gone

The Word of God says that the Spirit of God moved upon the face of the deep in Genesis 1. It says that the earth was at that time void, and darkness was upon the face of the deep. Then the Spirit of God moved, and God said, *"Let there be light."* Did you know that light never stops traveling? The light from our universe's creation is expanding; God spoke it into being. God is light.

When God speaks into you, He removes the darkness out of your life and replaces it with His light. Whenever you hear from Heaven, light replaces darkness in your body, mind, and spirit. Have you ever said, "It just dawned on me"? That was the light of God coming in. God was speaking. Before you were born again, you were without form and void. Darkness was upon the face of your deep. But the more God speaks to you, the more the light of God will show forth.

God's Voice – Your Darkness Gone

In Matthew 10:27 Jesus made a wonderful statement. He said, *"What I tell you in darkness, that speaks ye in light; and what ye hear in the ear, that preach ye upon the rooftops."* What does "What I tell you in the darkness" mean? Before the Father speaks, the area He addresses is filled with darkness and needs a revelation. When God speaks to that area it's filled with light. When darkness was upon the earth, God spoke light into existence. He said, "Let there be light." When He speaks into your life, He speaks into your darkness. His light comes in. You are to speak those things in the light. The darkness that held you in bondage can no longer hold you. You have been let out of the darkness, and now you are free in the light!

Then Jesus said, "And what ye hear in the ear, that preach ye upon the housetops." This is what the body of Christ needs to do. If the light you have been given from God is "Jesus loves me, this I know," then that is what you need to share. If the light you have received is from becoming a Christian, having God deal with your heart, and knowing you had to give your life over to Jesus, then that is what you need to share! The only things we need to shout from the rooftops is that which we have heard from our Father.

Speaking From the Voice

I want to share something personal with you that I discovered a long time ago. I have preached a lot of sermons that I did not receive from the Father. Instead, I had just heard someone else preach them, and I thought, "This is a good message; I am going to preach it." I have seen this done by a lot of other preachers as well, and I know that this practice can get you into trouble because you are sharing things for which you do not have a rock. The Word of God says that Jesus will build His church upon the rock, and the gates of hell cannot prevail against it. When you share things that the Father hasn't revealed to you personally, you could face some trouble because you do not have a rock to stand on.

We need to teach the Living Word every time we minister to someone; we need to tell them what the Father has shown to us. Upon this rock, our God is building His church, and the gates of hell will not prevail against it!

Section 3

Processing God's Voice

Chapter Nine

Unlocking the Mystery

N ow friends, let's begin to lay a foundation. In Mark 4:1-13, Jesus teaches a great multitude of people about the Kingdom of God. This principle is so powerful; He declares all doctrine to be based on understanding this parable. Mark 4: 1-13: *"And He began again to teach by the sea side: and there was gathered unto Him a great multitude, so that He entered into a ship, and sat in the sea; and the whole multitude was by the sea on the land. And He taught them many things by parables, and said unto them in His doctrine, Hearken; Behold, there went out a sower to sow: and it came to pass, as he sowed, some fell by the way side, and the fowls of the air came and devoured them up. And some fell on stony ground, where it had not much earth; and immediately it sprang up because it had no depth of earth: But when the sun was up, it was scorched; and because it had no root, it withered away. And some fell among thorns, and the thorns grew up, and choked it, and it yielded no fruit. And others fell on good ground, and did yield fruit that sprang up and increased; and brought forth, some thirty and some sixty and some a hundred. And He said unto them, He that hath ears to hear, let him hear. And when He was alone, the disciples who were about Him asked of Him the parable. And He said*

unto them, Unto you it is given to know the mystery of the kingdom of God: but unto them who are without, all these things are done in parables: That seeing they may see, and not perceive; and hearing they may hear, and not understand; lest at any time they should be converted, and their sins should be forgiven them. And He said unto them, Know ye not this parable? And how then will ye know all parables?"

This is one of the most important Scriptures in the Bible as far as understanding how the Kingdom of God works. However, there are only certain people who are able to comprehend it. God only reveals the mysteries of the Kingdom of God to those who seek Him with their whole heart. There are some things that are hidden from those who refuse to seek God. When God begins to draw someone unto Himself, that person has a choice to either submit to God or ignore Him. The difference between seeking God and ignoring Him is like that between playing a game or observing it from the sidelines. Please understand that faith in God is not a spectator's sport. He is the life your heart cries out for; He is the love you've been looking for. Our Heavenly Father is the only One who can fill the void within us. When you go after God with all your heart, life becomes exciting! Suddenly, God will begin to show you things; He will start revealing Himself to you. Your prayers – even the thoughts of your heart – will be answered. The apostle Paul in 1 Corinthians 2:9 describes this very miracle: *"...[The] eye has not seen, no ear has heard, and no mind has imagined what God has prepared for those who love Him."*

God desires you to know this: If you go after Him with your whole heart, He will begin to speak to you the very mysteries of God and the secrets of Heaven that will transform your life.

Jesus First

Jesus' disciples denied themselves and gave up their jobs, their land, their homes, and their families and came after Him with all of their hearts. God ought to be first place in our lives. He is second to no one. These men believed so strongly in Jesus and His message that they were willing to leave everything and follow Him.

He said, *"It's given to you to know the mystery of the Kingdom of God."* For those who are without (those not in relationship with God), He uses parables so that they may *"See and not perceive, and hearing they may not understand, least at any time they be converted and their sins forgiven of them."*

Isn't this amazing? The Bible says, *"Except the Father draw a man, he cannot be saved."* You would think that the Father would draw everyone. We see in 2 Corinthians 5:19 that God was in Christ Jesus drawing the world back to Himself. We know that it's not God's will that any perish; we know that He wants all of us saved. Did you know that God knows your heart? He knows you better than you know yourself. When He presents Himself to you, you have a seed sown in your heart. When the Father does this you get the chance to respond. If you submit to God and begin to seek Him, His words will begin to make sense to you. The key is to respond with your whole heart. Right now, as you are reading this, some of you are being drawn to God. He is speaking to your spirit and saying, "I love you, and I have a plan and a purpose for your life. Surrender everything to Me and I will begin to speak to you and reveal the mysteries of the Kingdom of God." How exciting is that? God desires to speak to each of us and give us the freedom to hear His voice.

Finding God's Plan

Now, salvation means to be born again, to be healed, to be delivered, to be set free, and to be blessed by God. John 10:10 reads: *"... I have come that they might have life, and that they might have it more abundantly."*

That life is the very life of the Father. God is saying "I'm going to bless you in this earth with My very life, and you're going to have a better life than you would have had if you had done this on your own." God has a life for you that will be much better than anything you can muster up on your own. Anything that you could possibly try to put together – all of your plans, all of your ideas – will not compare to what God's plan is for your life. God has a plan that is set into motion as you begin to hear His voice, and understand the mystery of the Kingdom of God.

You must respond to God pulling on your heart. Jesus says, *"If you come after Me with your whole heart, you will be able to see and understand the mystery of the Kingdom. Those who come after Me with their whole heart, those are the ones who will hear and understand. Those are the ones who will look and be able to see and perceive."* Jesus says in John 14:8, *"I am the way, the truth, and the life: no man cometh unto the Father, but by Me."* Then Jesus said in John 10:7, *"I am the door of the sheepfold."* Jesus is the door. There are many people who come to Jesus Christ, and they stop at the door. Did you know that we've been invited to come into His house? The key to His house is your heart. When you accept Jesus Christ as your Savior, you accept Him as your Lord and Savior...not just as your Savior. He wants to save you to the uttermost. He wants to save you totally and completely. What He has to have in order to do that is your whole heart: not half of your heart, but all of it, your whole heart! This is where you find yourself: a place so powerful and life changing that Jesus thought even His disciples – His followers – needed to know of it. The Father wants you to know much more, too. We have been given the opportunity to know the mysteries of the Kingdom of God. These mysteries are so profound and revolutionary that they unlock all the others. Praise God – that's powerful.

However, do you have permission to know the mysteries of the Kingdom of God? In Mark 4:14, Jesus explains what He has told to the multitudes. But friends, you still won't be able to understand unless you have entered into a personal relationship with God through Jesus Christ. I know people who have gone to the same church I've gone to, heard the same messages I've heard, and seen the same miracles of God that I've seen, and they still don't understand. I wonder, "How could they go through all of this and still not have a clue?" It's because until God has given you eyes to see – until He has given you the ability to look at what He is doing – you're going to miss it.

Chapter Ten

Kingdom Gardener

In John 15:1,[12c] Jesus makes the statement: *"I am the vine and you are the branches, and my Father is the husbandman."*Husbandman means gardener. Jesus is saying that the Father (God) is the gardener. God is the one who takes care of the garden in the Kingdom. So, you have to understand what a gardener does. The gardener is the one who tills the ground. The gardener makes sure the ground is good for sowing seed in. The gardener is the one who actually sows the seed. The gardener waters and makes sure the soil is healthy so that the seed will come forth properly. The gardener harvests the crop. **God is the gardener of the Kingdom of God.**

Man teaches us to clean ourselves. If you go to churches anywhere in the world, you may hear sermons of condemnation or guilt that cause you to want to repent or to run and hide. It's good to repent. But you could have a problem similar to the priests' problem in the Old Testament. The priest could not go into the holy of holies – the innermost sanctified room in the temple – if he had an evil conscience. Hebrews 9 shows that no one, not even the High Priest who went in once a year behind the veil, could go into the holiest of all because He had an evil conscience.

Today, a lot of church officials don't feel good about their services unless they have a certain number of people repent at the end of the service. But the other portion of the congregation is thinking, "Well, I repented last week and the week before so it's not necessary to do it this week." And before we know it, we could be stuck in a religious system of having men trying to cleanse the church by fixating on the notion of repentance, and this is God's job. I'll say it like this: I've never seen a fish jump into a boat, ask for a knife and say, "I'll take care of it." I've never seen a fish that, when caught, was already clean. Do you know what happens the minute we begin to try to clean ourselves? We begin to put on a façade – an image – that we call religion. Do you remember when Jesus said, *"You vipers and serpents"?* He said, *"You are full of a dead man's bones."* What is He saying? He is saying, "You're putting on a cover up, like you've been cleaning yourself, but deep down on the inside you are all messed up." This inner guilt and condemnation keeps the church from enjoying the fellowship with their heavenly Father. We have not understood why and how God would talk with us when we are so far from perfect. Jesus says in the Word that He is the way, the truth, and the life. Jesus says He is the only way to the Father. Jesus is our way to the Father and the Father's way to us. With Jesus you can come to know your God.

Understanding Kingdom Doctrine

"The sower soweth the word. And these are they by the way side, where the word is sown; but when they have heard, Satan cometh immediately, and taketh away the word that was sown in their hearts. And these are they likewise which are sown on stony ground; who, when they have heard the word, immediately receive it with gladness; And have no root in themselves, and so endure but for a time: afterward,

*when affliction or persecution ariseth for the word's sake,
immediately they are offended. And these are they which
are sown among thorns; such as hear the word, And the
cares of this world, and the deceitfulness of riches, and
the lusts of other things entering in, choke the word, and
it becometh unfruitful. And these are they which are sown
on good ground; such as hear the word, and receive it, and
bring forth fruit, some thirtyfold, some sixty, and some an
hundred." Mark 4:14-20*

Now, I want you to understand this: I have read many
great men and women of God interpret this parable as being
the difference between Christians and non-Christians. For
the purpose of instruction and exhortation (2 Timothy 3:16),
let us look at the verses in a different light, assuming that
every type of ground mentioned in Mark 4:14-20 represents
different types of believers - people already in relationship
with God. Romans 14:17 says, *"For the Kingdom of God
is not meat and drink; but righteousness, and peace, and
joy in the Holy Ghost."* Remember that you are the temple
of the Holy Spirit. Luke 17:21 says, *"The Kingdom of God
is in you."* The sower, the gardener, the husbandman, and
the Father speak into the Kingdom inside you. The Father
speaks into your life. When this happens, it's a powerful
thing. God speaks strength into your spirit. His thoughts
become your own and they are so strong, you can't deny
them – so strong that it will make you cry. God says, "I love
you." When God speaks, He is drawing you even closer to
Himself. The Kingdom of God is being revealed in you, and
life, as you know it, changes. When you read the Bible, and
God reveals things to you, the Kingdom of God will come
alive. John 16 tells us that the Holy Spirit only says that with
which He hears. Even Jesus said the words He spoke were
not His own. God is speaking. Remember, the restoration of
mankind is in rebuilding our relationship with God.

Chapter Eleven

Four Types of Believers

In Mark chapter 4, Jesus addresses the believer about the importance of understanding the principles of the Kingdom of God. Just because someone is a believer doesn't necessarily mean that they will bear fruit in every area of their life, let alone fruit that produces a harvest of thirty, sixty, or one hundredfold. The fruit in a believer's life is contingent upon the soil of their heart. In 1 Corinthians 3:11-15 the apostle Paul shares: *"For no other foundation can anyone lay than that which is laid, which is Jesus Christ. Now if anyone builds on this foundation with gold, silver, precious stones, wood, hay, or straw, each one's work will become clear; for the Day will declare it because it will be revealed by fire; and the fire will test each one's work of what sort it is. If anyone's work which he has built on it endures, he will receive a reward. If anyone's work is burned, he will suffer loss; but he himself will be saved, yet so as through fire."*

The apostle Paul is sharing that the foundation of our salvation is the blood of Jesus. It is what is laid upon this foundation that determines the fruit in a person's life: **our ability to hear, interpret, and obey what God says.** According to the Word of God there will be a day when everything that is laid upon the foundation of Jesus will be tried by fire. Only that which we have heard, interpreted, and obeyed will withstand the fire and produce fruit. Everything else will be consumed. Those things that God has spoken and not received properly will be burned up according to this passage even though the individual will be saved by the blood of Jesus.

In Mark 4:3-20 Jesus explains the parable of the sower. This story illustrates what will determine the fruit we produce when we learn to hear God's voice.

Wayside Ground

"And these are the ones by the wayside where the Word is sown. When they hear, satan comes immediately and takes away the Word that was sown into their hearts."
Mark 4:14

Let's take a look at the wayside ground Jesus referred to in Mark 4. When God speaks into the heart or spirit of a person in relationship with God, it is as though a seed were sown into the ground. The enemy cannot do anything about it. The devil can't stop God from speaking, and he can't stop a child of God from hearing. So the way the enemy tries to steal what God has said is by oppressing the soul and body. He wants to steal the Word that the Father has spoken to an individual's heart.

The soul of a man consists of his mind, will, emotions, and intellect. The Bible tells us in Romans 8:7 "that the carnal mind, or mind of the flesh, is at war with God." When God speaks into the heart of a carnal-minded child of God, he begins to argue with God based on his mind, will, emotions, and intellect. The carnal-minded person is still led by his senses – what he hears, sees, or feels, etc. Sometimes what God says will line up with what our mind, will, emotions, and intellect tell us, but other times it will not. It is during the times when our mind, will, emotions, and intellect are not in agreement that we must choose to be led by what God has spoken into our spirit. The devil would love for us to disregard what the Father is speaking. If the carnal mind of a child of God is fully active, it is easier for the enemy to convince him to let go of what God has said.

If we, as children of God, do not have our minds renewed by what God says through his Word and what He speaks personally to us, we're in trouble. We cannot overcome the storms in our lives if we don't know the perfect will of God. The devil would love for us to allow him to steal the seed of God's Word.

It is a lot easier to believe that God will provide financing if I know what His will is on a matter. In Philippians 4:19 it says that "He supplies all my needs according to His riches in glory," and when God makes that alive in my spirit it becomes easier for me to believe Him when my bank account is in the red. As it says in Ephesians 4:23, God will help you *"To be renewed in the spirit of your mind."* Romans 12:2 tells us: *"To be transformed by the renewing of your mind, that you may prove what is the good, the acceptable, and the perfect will of God."*

If you don't want to be *wayside ground*, you must have your mind renewed by God and it must be renovated to help you think as He does. This is a choice. You can choose to believe what God says regardless of the circumstances around you. You can choose to love everyone. You can choose to forgive everyone. You can choose to put God first in everything. When you choose the way of God, you will no longer be influenced by your circumstances because your mind will be opened to God's voice. He can then begin the transformation process and move you closer and closer to His perfect will.

Galatians 5:19-21 tells us that there are certain things that will prevent us from living a Spirit-controlled life. These things are described as the works of man's flesh that keep a person from operating and living in the blessings of God. They are *"Adultery, fornication, uncleanness, lasciviousness, idolatry, sorcery, hatred, contentions, jealousies, outbursts of wrath, selfish ambitions, dissentions, heresies, envyings, murders, drunkenness, revelings, and the like. I tell you now that those who practice such things will not inherit the Kingdom of God."*

When God speaks to a child of God influenced by the flesh, it is easy for the devil to influence him, to let go of what God has said. Galatians 5:25 reads: *"If we live in the Spirit, let us also walk in the Spirit."*

Let me make something clear. If you have given your life to Jesus and are a child of God, you can live in the Spirit and still not walk in the Spirit. Being in relationship with God doesn't automatically guarantee that we walk in the Spirit. We have to prevent ourselves from walking in the flesh. However, Galatians 5:16 tells us how we can overcome our flesh and become ground that can hear and bring forth what God is saying. *"I say unto you, walk in the Spirit, and you will not fulfill the lust of the flesh."*

Again, if you will choose to seek God with all your heart, to pray and seek God's face and become a student of His Word, and allow God's love to overflow in you, then the desires of your flesh will begin to be suppressed and your heavenly Father will reign in you. Then, when your Father speaks to you, the devil's influence will be broken from your life. You can hear and bring forth what God has said to you.

God will speak to you about everything in life – marriage, children, jobs, money, housing and transportation. God is life! God will speak and bring forth your victory. In every one of these areas and more, life is better with God.

Stony Ground

"These likewise are the ones sown on stony ground who,
when they hear the Word, immediately receive it with
gladness; and they have no root in themselves, and so
endure only for a time. Afterward when tribulation or
persecution arises for the Word's sake,
immediately they stumble." Mark 4:16-17

Stony ground is exciting ground. When the Father speaks to this type of believer, he gets very excited and tells everyone what God has said. This believer usually displays a lot of emotion, but never brings forth what the Father has spoken to him. Jesus says this is because there are no roots in the ground. This child of God is easily offended when afflictions and persecutions come. When the enemy comes to steal the Word that God has spoken to his heart, his pride is hurt and he is distracted from God's work.

Proverbs 16:18 tells us that, pride goes before destruction – a haughty spirit before a fall. Pride sets you up for failure. You like people to know that God is talking to you. You want everyone to know what He has said, but at the first point of opposition you're offended and embarrassed, and let what the Father spoke to you fall to the ground. You must be humble and not let pride get in the way of your relationship with God. Let your roots grow deep with God by denying your carnal self. It's exciting to wait with patience for what God promised.

Thorns

"Now these are the ones sown among thorns; they are the
ones that hear the Word, and the cares of this world,
the deceitfulness of riches, and the desires for other
things entering in choke the Word,
and it becomes unfruitful." Mark 4:18-19

This type of believer is full of thorns – cares of this world, deceitfulness of riches, and lust of other things. When God speaks, the enemy uses the thorns to choke the Word to the point that it isn't able to produce fruit. This believer really needs to get into the Word of God and practice what it says to get rid of those thorns. *"Be doers of the Word and not hearers only, or you will be self-deceived"* Run into your heavenly Father's arms, and fall in love with Him, and trust Him with your life.

How do you remove thorns? The cares of this world are worry; anxiety and fear, and they can rule your life. Don't try to solve every problem yourself or to control the situation. When you don't have the solution, don't panic and worry. It won't help. You need to trust God. God's solution is 1 Peter 5:6-7: *"Humble yourself under the mighty hand of God, that He may exalt you in due time: casting all your care upon Him, for He cares for you."* God's solution is for you to stop trusting yourself and put your trust in Him. Stop letting the thorn of worry rob your relationship with God.

The deceitfulness of riches and worrying about riches is also a problem in the body of Christ. This child of God wants to make sure that what God promised Him is in his budget. God's promises are empowered by God's riches and everything is His, so nothing is impossible with Him. Don't let money be the hurdle between you and what God has waiting for you. He is a giver and has placed in His children a giving nature. Sometimes all you have is the vision and the Word of God spoken to you and that is all you need to enter into what God has called you to do.

In order to see the Word overcome the deceitfulness of riches, give your whole heart to God. Matthew 6:21 says, *"Where your treasure is, there your heart will be also."* Money is not the real problem. You will always move forward with what God says if He has your whole heart. Become a faithful giver, and watch God bring victory forth through what He speaks to you.

Lust of other things does not have to be for sinful things. It can be an ungodly lust for sports, shopping, family, or anything that becomes more important than Him. If you are trying to enjoy something that you know you need to give up, don't be surprised when you can't operate in what the Father has told you.

You need to fall in love with God – make Him first place in your life, and seek Him first. Matthew 6:33 says, *"But seek ye first the Kingdom of God, and all His righteousness and all these things will be added unto you."* God will satisfy your needs as you follow after Him. Give up your other gods in order to see God's victory in your life. Do you really believe that what you have is better than what God can give you? Understand what is available to you. God is so incredible. He is greater than anything you can imagine.

Good Ground

"But these are the ones sown on good ground, those who hear the Word, accept it and bear fruit; some thirtyfold, some sixty, some a hundred." Mark 4:20

A heart that receives what God says and brings forth productive fruit – this is what we all want to be. I like success. I like to see things through to victory. So how do we become good ground? God speaks; I receive it, and I bring it forth. I receive what God says, and I bring it forth. Some people think that living in faith is just saying, "I believe." They want God to give them things that He hasn't necessarily promised. But the Scripture notes that when God says something, we hear what He says, and we bring it forth. There is labor included here. If you have been called to run a homeless shelter then you may not live a life of luxury. We all have responsibilities, problems, and bills to pay. If you pastor a church, you'll have work to do as well. You are not delivered from anything. Living by faith does not give you the right to be lazy. God wants to see that we will put an effort towards what we need.

Hundredfold

I don't know about you, but I want the fruits of my life to be one hundredfold. How many times have you walked towards something that God showed you a vision of, but when it came to fruition, it wasn't as large as what God had shown you? Why was it so scaled down? Well, Scripture tells us in Mark 4:24, *"And He said unto them, take heed what ye hear: with what measure ye mete, it shall be measured to you: and unto you that hear, shall more be given. For he that hath, to him shall be given: and he that hath not, from him shall be taken, even that which he hath."*

When God speaks to you, take heed of what He says. When God tells me something, I repeat it back to Him. That's my acknowledgement. That's my way of taking heed. The Scripture also notes that the way in which you measure it is the way in which you will receive it. Then let us measure it the way God speaks it because His ideas are so much higher than ours. God says, for example, "I'm going to save your whole neighborhood." And you tell people exactly what you've heard because you believe it. Three months later, someone asks you, "How many of your neighbors have been saved?" and you answer, "Well, I haven't heard of anybody right now, but God said He would save everybody on my block." What you have done is measured it down, from your entire neighborhood getting saved, to only one block getting saved. Then one neighbor is saved and you say, "Wow, God told me that *one of my neighbors* was going to get saved." You measured it down from your neighborhood getting saved to one block, and then you measured it down from one block getting saved to just one neighbor. That's what we do. We are so worried about us and the way we think, and the way we look, that we take God's Word and we measure it down.

God says, "I know you are human, I know you are flesh. As long as you take My Word and it brings forth something, then I will continue to speak to you." But we ought to desire to see everything that God has said in its fullness! We need to begin measuring it right. It's the whole neighborhood! It's not just one neighbor. God said it. Why not believe Him for what He is saying?

There have been instances in my life when God has spoken something in my spirit so strongly that I couldn't shake it, but as I began to share it with people it was measured down. In Matthew 7:6 Jesus says, "Don't cast your pearls before swine." What is He saying? He will speak things to you that are specifically for you and the people you trust, but He cautions you to use discernment. Others may not be able to understand what you have heard and they may measure it down so hold it close!

God says, *"For he that hath, to him shall be given; and he that hath not, from him shall be taken, even that which he hath."* He says, I'm going to bless you more; I'm going to talk to you more. Would you like God to start speaking to you more? The more that you receive, the more God is going to talk. Then the Bible goes on to say "and he that hath not, from him shall be taken, even that which he hath." What does this mean? It is a gentle warning that if you don't receive what He says and bring it forth He will take it away. I don't want God to stop talking to me. I want to hear more and more and more. We ought to choose, no matter what, to always measure what God says exactly the way He has said it.

Section 4

The Fullness of God

Chapter Twelve

Rain from Heaven

*"For My thoughts are not your thoughts, neither are your
ways My ways," declares the LORD. "As the heavens are
higher than the earth, so are My ways higher than your
ways and My thoughts than your thoughts. As the rain and
the snow come down from Heaven, and do not return to it,
without watering the earth and making it bud and flourish,
so that it yields seed for the sower and bread for the eater,
so is My Word that goes out from My mouth: It will not
return to Me empty, but will accomplish what I desire and
achieve – the purpose for which I sent it." Isaiah 55:8-11*

Can you imagine hearing from God so much that it feels
like rain? The God of this Universe desires to talk
personally to me, Spirit to spirit, all the time. God is bringing
forth a glorious church. We know that this church is being
made glorious by the cleansing water of the Word, both the
letter and the *spoken Word.*

God's Drawing
If you are born again as God's child, you have heard Him
speak to you. The Bible says a man is only saved if the Father
draws him. "I am the way the truth and the life and no man

comes to the Father but by Me." The Holy Spirit was upon you, and the Father came and drew you to Jesus Christ. Isn't it good how powerful the blood of Jesus is? God Himself can come draw you into His house.

Encouraging Words

We're on our way to seeing what God is going to do and what He is already doing. This is a great time for the church. God spoke to me concerning the church, and said that those who have been willing to die to self and come after Him through the years; He said that He is going to pour His glory out on them and He's going to bless the church. The *Glory* means to be weighted down with everything good and to shine with splendor. Then He spoke another thing to me, like what's stated in Romans chapter 11 (when He speaks about blessing the gentile church so greatly that it would provoke Israel to jealously so much that they will be saved), He said that He was going to take those who have denied themselves and have come after Him fervently, those who have loved Him with all of their heart, and He's going to bless them – to the point that those around them will be envious and jealous of what they have. It's time for the heathen to come to the Lord. God said that He would give us the heathen as our inheritance. We're going to get our inheritance because He is blessing those who have been faithful to Him. Are you one of them? You can't confess to be faithful – you either are or you aren't. It's not too late to come after God with all of your heart and let Him work in your life.

God Saw Us

In Hosea 6:1-2 it says: *"Come, and let us return unto the LORD for He hath torn, and He will heal us; He hath smitten, and He will bind us up. After two days will He revive us; on the third day He will raise us up, and we shall live in His sight."*

Do you understand that we are partakers with Jesus Christ in His death, burial, and resurrection? Did you know that in the Spirit there is no time or distance? The glorious church can be caught up in the twinkling of an eye – because there is no time or distance in the Spirit. I'm telling you that God has things he can do before the blink of an eye. Look at 2 Corinthians 12:2-3: *"I knew a man in Christ above fourteen years ago, (whether in the body, I cannot tell; or whether out of the body, I cannot tell: God knoweth) such an one caught up to the third heaven. And I knew such a man, (whether in the body, or out of the body, I cannot tell: God knoweth)."*

Paul said he didn't know how it happened; He just knew he was there. Why? Because there is no time or distance in the Spirit. That's right. When God separated the light from darkness, He caused them to work together to give us the first day. God created time to work in the natural realm. Jesus Christ was born into time. He is the Alpha and Omega, the beginning, and the end. Jesus is the Word God spoke when He said let there be light and He is the Word in the grand finale that returns on a white horse with the armies of God. However God lives in eternity and this whole world is returning to eternity. In eternity there will be no more night and day, no more time. We will all live in the pure light of God. Revelation 22:5-6 says, *"And there shall be no night there; and they need no candle, neither light of the sun; for the Lord God giveth them light: and they shall reign for ever and ever. And he said unto me, these sayings are faithful and true: and the Lord God of the holy prophets sent his angel to shew unto his servants the things which must shortly be done."*

Hosea prophesies of the things Jesus would go through, but he talks as though we were going through them ourselves. Jesus was our substitute – He took our place. When Jesus was on the cross He was taking our punishment, and Hosea sees it as though we were on the cross. He also sees us in the resurrection. In eternity when Jesus was on the cross God saw us on the cross; when Jesus died He saw us die, and when Jesus rose from the dead, He saw us raised from the dead. Ephesians 2:4-6 confirms this to be true. In eternity your salvation happened at the same time as Jesus' death, burial, and resurrection.

He's Coming As Rain

Now let's look at Hosea chapter 6, verse 3: *"Then shall we know, if we follow on to know the Lord."* I have to say this...if you don't follow on to know Him, to seek to know the Lord with your whole heart, and fellowship with Him, then you won't know what God is doing. But if you follow on to know Him, then it says; *"His going forth is prepared as the morning."*

He is going to let you in on what He is doing. Ask Him. He is going to let you begin to understand the plans He has for you. Ask Him. He is going to order your steps, and you're not going to be blind to the things that He has for you. Ask Him to show you. Isn't this good news? The quote refers to the body of Christ (the church). Then it says: *"And He shall come unto us as the rain; as the latter and former rain unto the earth."*

There's that word, *rain*, again. He says that He is going to come at you like the rain. How does this rain compare to the rain in Isaiah 55? He said: *"So shall My Word be"* and He said, *"I'm going to send Him as the rain."*

That's what I love. "I'm going to send Him as the rain." Jesus is the manifestation of the former and latter rain. He came and fulfilled the Word of the old covenant, and he is the Word of the new covenant. He is what God has said and is everything that God will say. Jesus is the Word made flesh that lived among us. Jesus is the WORD! This helps us to understand what God is waiting on in this Scripture. James 5:7 says: *"Be patient therefore, brethren, unto the coming of the Lord. Behold, the husbandman waiteth for the precious fruit of the earth, and hath long patience for it, until he receive the early and latter rain."*

Now this is a powerful statement. First of all, He tells us to be patient and then it says that the husbandman has long patience. Do you remember who the husbandman is? The Bible says in John 15: *"I am the vine and you are the branches and my Father is the husbandman."*

The Bible says that we don't know the day or the hour when Jesus will come back for us. Jesus Himself doesn't know the day or the hour, only God does, and He is obviously waiting for something. The long patience isn't for natural events to happen, but for the manifestation of the works that God has started in us. Jesus was the fulfiller of the Old Covenant and He is the Word and mediator of the New Covenant. Jesus said that man should not live on bread alone, but by every Word that comes out of the mouth of God. Jesus is the bread of life, but He is also the Word. We must have both the Bible and the spoken Word of the Lord.

James 5 shows us that God is waiting on something. He is waiting until He receives the early and the latter rain. God sent it, and He is waiting to receive it. Jesus Christ came to us as the former and the latter rain and now He is waiting for a church (the body of Christ) that is established in the *written Word,* but is also hearing the spoken Word.

Jesus Manifested

We need to be established in the truths of God's Word. *"He was wounded for our transgressions; He was bruised for our iniquities, and the chastisement of our peace was upon Him, and by His stripes we are healed." "My God shall supply all of your needs according to His riches and glory in Christ Jesus."* Its God will for you to prosper and be in health, even as your soul prospers. He who bears our sins upon His own body that we being dead to sin, should live unto righteousness, by whose stripes we are healed. Bless the Lord, oh my soul, and forget not all of His benefits, who forgives all our iniquities, who heals all of our diseases. These truths are meant to be coupled with hearing from God. We must know God personally. Jesus was sent to Calvary to establish a way for us to fellowship with God. The Bible says, *"Know ye not that you're the temple of the Holy Spirit,"* and *"Know ye not that you're the temple of God?"* God is waiting to see Jesus manifested in you. He's waiting to see the former and latter rain in you. He's waiting to see people who are established in the Bible and are walking in the Spirit. He's looking for people who are established in the truth and are walking after the Spirit of God, and who know their God.

Chapter Fourteen

Water to Wine

When Jesus showed up at the wedding in Cana, His mother said *"There is no wine,"* Jesus' mother is making a demand on Him. Jesus' is asking, *"What do you want Me to do? It's not My hour; it's not My wedding day."* Mary turns around and says, *"Whatsoever He says, do it."* This is how the last day church will operate.

There are six water pots and Jesus wants them filled to the brim with water. *"Now you are cleaned by the water of the Word."* *"As the rain comes down and watereth the earth, so shall My Word be that goeth out of My mouth."* The water represents the Word. Jesus told the servants to dip into the water pots, and the water turned into wine. Wine represents the fullness of God. When we became believers, man started filling us to the brim with His written Word. Out of hunger and thirst to know Him we studied our Bibles and we listened to CDs; we have attended seminars and conferences. We have been filling ourselves with the Word of God. Now He is turning the water into wine, and making us the fullness of God. He is igniting a move of His Spirit; He is igniting a people who are hearing God. They are having dreams and visions, the like of which they've never had before. Jesus is being formed in us. Now Jesus will be seen on the earth as He was seen before, but this time through the Bride.

Bright Clouds

This is a great day to be alive. Do you realize how many people on the face of the earth are now hearing His Word and believing His Word today? If He hasn't yet dipped into you, then He is about to; just get ready. Let's read Zechariah 10:1: *"Ask ye of the LORD rain in the time of the latter rain; so the LORD shall make bright clouds, and give them showers of rain, to every one grass in the field."*

What is going on here? He is saying that during this time of the latter rain, you ought to be praying for rain. You should be saying, "God I want to hear You more than ever; I want to know Your voice; I want to know what You're saying to me; I need Your direction; speak into my heart and my life; show me God, show me God; I'm hungry and thirsty; I want to know You; I want to know Your voice; I want Your thoughts to come into me and strengthen me time and time again, so that I can be one who You work through. He said that during this time of the latter rain, we need to pray for rain, and He said, "I'll tell you what I'll do; I'll send bright clouds." What is this? It is the men and women of God who are hearing His voice. Men and women of God who aren't just preaching the written Word, but who are getting up and saying, "God said this," and "God is showing me that," and "Look at what this means." These actions are bringing revelation to the body of Christ and it's as though they were dipping into the water pots. God is doing it. So He said, "Pray and I'll send bright clouds and they are going to send showers of rain to you." They're going to hear what I'm saying and they are going to pass the words on to you. They are going to stir you up to hear God yourself. They're going to stir you up to press into God. It's a great day; it's a day of rain. You see the rain is here; it's already here. Just say, "God give me more, give me more." Let Jesus be formed in me; let the former and latter rain be formed in me. I don't want to be holding His coming back. I want to be filled with Your Word and filled with Your presence.

You Are Valuable

Isn't this powerful? With this in mind, you're a container, you're a vessel. You're a high dollar vessel because if you've been born again, the highest price that has ever been paid for anything was paid for you. So for you to walk around as though you're not worthy is denying what He has paid for you. What's been paid for you is the Son of God, the Lamb of God who was slain before the foundations of the earth. His blood was shed for you. He suffered for you. He came and took on the form of man so that He could manifest God's love and desire for you. You may say "Well, I'm unworthy!" On our own merit we are, but we've been made worthy by the blood of the Lamb (Jesus Christ). This is a grace thing. It's not our own ability. If it's my own ability, then I need to stop trying myself because I'm about to get into trouble. How many times have you messed up operating out of your own ability? I wouldn't dare preach within my own ability. You better know your God and you better have trust in His amazing grace because it's His ability you're tapping into. It's what Jesus has done for you that enables all of this. Let's stand together in God's amazing grace. Seek His face and fulfill our God-given purpose. This whole thing is God's idea, bought and paid for with His Son Jesus Christ.

Kurnool responds to the Gospel.

The children at the Matthew 10/Miriam Children's Home.

Woman testifying of God's healing power.

Crowds of people coming to the altar to give their lives to Jesus Christ at a Matthew 10 Redemption Festival.

Dr. Pete presenting the Gospel in Warangal.

Precious women of God stricken with leprosy.

Dr. Pete proclaiming the Gospel of the Lord Jesus Christ.

**Dr. Pete greeting some of his children that were
victims of the 2004 tsunami.**

Young orphan giving praise to God.

**Truckload of people from a nearby city travel to
the Redemption Festival to hear
the Good News of Jesus!**

Widow praying at Redemption Festival in Nellore.

**Dr. Pete praying for a little girl
at the children's home.**

Thousands wave their decision cards in the air after giving their lives to Christ!

Dr. Pete ministering to the pastors.

Dr. Pete ministering to the widows.

Dr. Pete ministering to the children.

Scripture Foundation for Fellowshipping with His Voice

This next session is a reference point for you to use as you enter into a deeper fellowship with your Heavenly Father through Jesus Christ.

The following passages are descriptions that God and man have given to His voice. These examples will allow you to have a reference point in familiarizing yourself with God's voice.

Deuteronomy 4:12
And the **LORD** spoke to you out of the midst of the fire. You heard the sound of the words, but saw no form; you only heard a **voice**.

Deuteronomy 5:22
"These words the **LORD** spoke to all your assembly, in the mountain from the midst of the fire, the cloud, and the thick darkness, with a loud **voice**; and He added no more. And He wrote them on two tablets of stone and gave them to me.

1 Kings 19:12
and after the earthquake a fire, but the **LORD** was not in the fire; and after the fire a still small **voice**.

Psalm 29:3
The **voice** of the **LORD** is over the waters; the God of glory thunders; The **LORD** is over many waters.

Psalm 29:4
The **voice** of the **LORD** is powerful; the **voice** of the **LORD** is full of majesty.

Psalm 29:5
The **voice** of the **LORD** breaks the cedars, Yes, the **LORD** splinters the cedars of Lebanon.

Psalm 29:7
The **voice** of the **LORD** divides the flames of fire.

Psalm 29:8

The **voice** of the **LORD** shakes the wilderness; The **LORD** shakes the Wilderness of Kadesh.

Psalm 29:9

The **voice** of the **LORD** makes the deer give birth, And strips the forests bare; And in His temple everyone says, "Glory!"

Psalm 12:6

The **word**s of the **LORD** are pure **word**s, like silver tried in a furnace of earth, Purified seven times.

Psalm 18:30

As for God, His way is perfect; the **word** of the **LORD** is proven; He is a shield to all who trust in Him.

Psalm 33:4

For the **word** of the **LORD** is right, and all His work is done in truth.

In the entire book of Genesis we see that God had a lot to say in regards to His creation, His covenants with man, and with the men involved in those covenants. The following passages will better familiarize you with the Voice of God throughout creation and His first dealings with man.

Genesis 1:3

*Then **God said**, "Let there be light"; and there was light.*

Genesis 1:6

*Then **God said**, "Let there be a firmament in the midst of the waters, and let it divide the waters from the waters."*

Genesis 1:11

*Then **God said**, "Let the earth bring forth grass, the herb that yields seed, and the fruit tree that yields fruit according to its kind, whose seed is in itself, on the earth"; and it was so. Then **God said**, "Let there be a firmament in the midst of the waters, and let it divide the waters from the waters."*

Genesis 1:9

*Then **God said**, "Let the waters under the heavens be gathered together into one place, and let the dry land appear"; and it was so.*

Genesis 1:14

*Then **God said**, "Let there be lights in the firmament of the heavens to divide the day from the night; and let them be for signs and seasons, and for days and years;*

Genesis 1:20
*Then **God said**, "Let the waters abound with an abundance of living creatures, and let birds fly above the earth across the face of the firmament of the heavens."*

Genesis 1:24
*Then **God said**, "Let the earth bring forth the living creature according to its kind: cattle and creeping thing and beast of the earth, each according to its kind"; and it was so.*

Genesis 1:26
*Then **God said**, "Let Us make man in Our image, according to Our likeness; let them have dominion over the fish of the sea, over the birds of the air, and over the cattle, over all the earth and over every creeping thing that creeps on the earth."*

Genesis 1:28
*Then **God** blessed them, and **God said** to them, "Be fruitful and multiply; fill the earth and subdue it; have dominion over the fish of the sea, over the birds of the air, and over every living thing that moves on the earth.*

Genesis 1:29
*And **God said**, "See, I have given you every herb that yields seed which is on the face of all the earth, and every tree whose fruit yields seed; to you it shall be for food.*

Genesis 2:18

*And the LORD **God said**, "It is not good that man should be alone; I will make him a helper comparable to him."*

Genesis 3:3

*But of the fruit of the tree which is in the midst of the garden, **God** has **said**, 'You shall not eat it, nor shall you touch it, lest you die.'"*

Genesis 3:8

And they heard the voice of the LORD God walking in the garden in the cool of the day: and Adam and his wife hid themselves from the presence of the LORD God amongst the trees of the garden.

Genesis 3:9

*Then the LORD **God** called to Adam and **said** to him, "Where are you?"*

Genesis 3:13

*And the LORD **God said** to the woman, "What is this you have done?" The woman **said**, "The serpent deceived me, and I ate."*

Genesis 3:14

*So the LORD **God said** to the serpent: "Because you have done this, You are cursed more than all cattle, And more than every beast of the field; On your belly you shall go, And you shall eat dust All the days of your life.*

Genesis 3:22

*Then the LORD **God said**, "Behold, the man has become like one of us, to know good and evil. And* *now, lest he put out his hand and take also of the tree of life, and eat, and live forever"*

Genesis 6:13

*[The Ark Prepared] And **God said** to Noah, "The end of all flesh has come before Me, for the earth is filled with violence through them; and behold, I will destroy them with the earth.*

Genesis 9:1

*So **God** blessed Noah and his sons, and **said** to them: "Be fruitful and multiply, and fill the earth.*

Genesis 9:12

*And **God said**: "This is the sign of the covenant which I make between Me and you, and every living creature that is with you, for perpetual generations.*

Genesis 17:1

*[The Sign of the Covenant] When Abram was ninety-nine years old, the LORD appeared to Abram and **said** to him, "I am Almighty **God**; walk before Me and be blameless.*

Genesis 17:9

*And **God said** to Abraham: "As for you, you shall keep My covenant, you and your descendants after you throughout their generations.*

Genesis 17:15

*Then **God said** to Abraham, "As for Sarai your wife, you shall not call her name Sarai, but Sarah shall be her name.*

Genesis 17:19

*Then **God said**: "No, Sarah your wife shall bear you a son, and you shall call his name Isaac; I will establish My covenant with him for an everlasting covenant, and with his descendants after him.*

Genesis 17:23

*So Abraham took Ishmael his son, all who were born in his house and all who were bought with his money, every male among the men of Abraham's house, and circumcised the flesh of their foreskins that very same day, as **God** had **said** to him.*

Genesis 20:3

*But **God** came to Abimelech in a dream by night, and **said** to him, "Indeed you are a dead man because of the woman whom you have taken, for she is a man's wife."*

Genesis 20:6

*And **God said** to him in a dream, "Yes, I know that you did this in the integrity of your heart. For I also withheld you from sinning against Me; therefore I did not let you touch her.*

Genesis 21:12

*But **God said** to Abraham, "Do not let it be displeasing in your sight because of the lad or because of your bondwoman. Whatever Sarah has **said** to you, listen to her voice; for in Isaac your seed shall be called.*

Genesis 21:17

*And **God** heard the voice of the lad. Then the angel of **God** called to Hagar out of heaven, and **said** to her,*

*"What ails you, Hagar? Fear not, for **God** has heard the voice of the lad where he is.*

Genesis 22:1

*[Abraham's Faith Confirmed] Now it came to pass after these things that **God** tested Abraham, and said to him, "Abraham!" And he said, "Here I am."*

Genesis 22:8

*And Abraham **said**, "My son, **God** will provide for Himself the lamb for a burnt offering." So the two of them went together.*

Genesis 26:24

*And the **LORD** appeared to him the same night and **said**, "I am the **God** of your father Abraham; do not fear, for I am with you. I will bless you **and** multiply your descendants for My servant Abraham's sake."*

Genesis 28:13

*And behold, the **LORD** stood above it and **said:** "I am the LORD **God** of Abraham your father and the **God** of Isaac; the land on which you lie I will give to you and your descendants.*

Genesis 31:16

*For all these riches which **God** has taken from our father are really ours and our children's; now then, whatever **God** has **said** to you, do it.*

Genesis 31:24

*But **God** had come to Laban the Syrian in a dream by night, and **said** to him, "Be careful that you speak to Jacob neither good nor bad."*

Genesis 32:9

Then Jacob said, "O God of my father Abraham and God of my father Isaac, the LORD who said to me, 'Return to your country and to your family, and I will deal well with you'

Genesis 32:28

And He said, "Your name shall no longer be called Jacob, but Israel; for you have struggled with God and with men, and have prevailed.

Genesis 35:1

[Jacob's Return to Bethel] Then God said to Jacob, "Arise, go up to Bethel and dwell there; and make an altar there to God, who appeared to you when you fled from the face of Esau your brother."

Genesis 35:10

And God said to him, "Your name is Jacob; your name shall not be called Jacob anymore, but Israel shall be your name." So He called his name Israel.

Genesis 35:11

Also God said to him: "I am God Almighty. Be fruitful and multiply; a nation and a company of nations shall proceed from you, and kings shall come from your body.

Genesis 41:25

Then Joseph said to Pharaoh, "The dreams of Pharaoh are one; God has shown Pharaoh what He is about to do:

Genesis 46:2

*Then **God** spoke to Israel in the visions of the night, and **said**, "Jacob, Jacob!" And he **said**, "Here I am."*

Genesis 46:3

*So He **said**, "I am **God**, the **God** of your father; do not fear to go down to Egypt, for I will make of you a great nation there.*

The following scriptures are examples of God talking to man throughout the Old and New Testaments.

Deuteronomy 4:12
*And the **LORD** spoke to you out of the midst of the fire. You **heard** the sound of the words, but saw no form; you only **heard** a **voice**.*

Deuteronomy 5:24
*And you said: 'Surely the **LORD** our God has shown us His glory and His greatness, and we have **heard** His **voice** from the midst of the fire. We have seen this day that God speaks with man; yet he still lives.*

Deuteronomy 5:28
*"Then the **LORD** **heard** the **voice** of your words when you spoke to me, and the **LORD** said to me: 'I have **heard** the **voice** of the words of this people which they have spoken to you. They are right in all that they have spoken.*

Deuteronomy 4:12
*And the **LORD** spoke to you out of the midst of the fire. You **heard** the sound of the words, but saw no form; you only **heard** a **voice**.*

Deuteronomy 5:24
*And you said: 'Surely the **LORD** our God has shown us His glory and His greatness, and we have **heard** His **voice** from the midst of the fire. We have seen this day that God speaks with man; yet he still lives.*

Deuteronomy 5:28
*"Then the **LORD** **heard** the **voice** of your words when you spoke to me, and the **LORD** said to me:*

*'I have **heard** the **voice** of the words of this people which they have spoken to you. They are right in all that they have spoken.*

Isaiah 6:8

*Also I **heard** the **voice** of the **Lord**, saying: "Whom shall I send, And who will go for Us?" Then I said, "Here am I! Send me."*

Isaiah 30:30

*The **LORD** will cause His glorious **voice** to be **heard**, and show the descent of His arm, With the indignation of His anger And the flame of a devouring fire, With scattering, tempest, and hailstone.*

Revelation 14:13

*Then I **heard** a **voice** from heaven saying to me, "Write: 'Blessed are the dead who die in the **Lord** from now on.'" "Yes," says the Spirit, "that they may rest from their labors, and their works follow them."*

Ezekiel 3:24

*Then the **Spirit** entered me and set me on my feet, and spoke with me and **said** to me: "Go, shut yourself inside your house.*

Ezekiel 11:5

*Then the **Spirit** of the LORD fell upon me, and **said** to me, "Speak! 'Thus says the LORD: "Thus you have **said**, O house of Israel; for I know the things that come into your mind.*

Zechariah 4:6

*So he answered and **said** to me: "This is the word of the LORD to Zerubbabel: ' Not by might nor by power, but by My **Spirit**,' Says the LORD of hosts.*

Luke 3:22

*And the Holy **Spirit** descended in bodily form like a dove upon Him, and a voice came from heaven which **said**, "You are My beloved Son; in You I am well pleased."*

Acts 8:29

*Then the **Spirit said** to Philip, "Go near and overtake this chariot."*

Acts 10:19

*While Peter thought about the vision, the **Spirit said** to him, "Behold, three men are seeking you.*

Acts 11:16

*Then I remembered the word of the Lord, how He **said**, 'John indeed baptized with water, but you shall be baptized with the Holy **Spirit**.'*

Acts 13:2

*As they ministered to the Lord and fasted, the Holy **Spirit said**, "Now separate to Me Barnabas and Saul for the work to which I have called them."*

Deuteronomy 4:12

*And the **LORD** spoke to you out of the midst of the fire. You heard the sound of the words, but saw no form; you only heard a **voice**.*

Deuteronomy 5:22

*"These words the **LORD** spoke to all your assembly, in the mountain from the midst of the fire, the cloud, and the thick darkness, with a loud **voice**; and He added no more. And He wrote them on two tablets of stone and gave them to me.*

Deuteronomy 5:24

*And you said: 'Surely the **LORD** our God has shown us His glory and His greatness, and we have heard His **voice** from the midst of the fire. We have seen this day that God speaks with man; yet he still lives.*

Judges 2:20

*Then the anger of the **LORD** was hot against Israel; and He said, "Because this nation has transgressed My covenant which I commanded their fathers, and has not heeded My **voice**,*

Judges 6:10

*Also I said to you, "I am the **LORD** your God; do not fear the gods of the Amorites, in whose land you dwell." But you have not obeyed My **voice**.*

Isaiah 6:8

*Also I heard the **voice** of the Lord, saying: "Whom shall I send, and who will go for us?" Then I said, "Here am I! Send me."*

Isaiah 31:4

*[God Will Deliver Jerusalem] For thus the **LORD** has spoken to me: " As a lion roars, And a young lion over his prey (When a multitude of shepherds is summoned against him, He will not be afraid of their **voice** Nor be disturbed by their noise), So the **LORD***

of hosts will come down To fight for Mount Zion and for its hill.

Jeremiah 3:12

Go and proclaim these words toward the north, and say: 'Return, backsliding Israel,' says the LORD; 'I will not cause My anger to fall on you. For I am merciful,' says the LORD; 'I will not remain angry forever. That you have transgressed against the LORD your God, and have scattered your charms to alien deities under every green tree, and you have not obeyed My voice,' says the LORD.

In all but one Epistle, the Apostle Paul introduces each book with a greeting: directly from God the Father and His Son Jesus Christ. These are the following scripture references.

Galatians 1:3

*Grace to you and peace from God the **Father** and our **Lord** Jesus Christ,*

Ephesians 1:2

*Grace to you and peace from God our **Father** and the **Lord** Jesus Christ.*

Ephesians 6:23

*Peace to the brethren, and love with faith, from God the **Father** and the **Lord** Jesus Christ.*

Philippians 1:2

*Grace to you and peace from God our **Father** and the **Lord** Jesus Christ.*

Colossians 1:2

*To the saints and faithful brethren in Christ who are in Colosse: Grace to you and peace from God our **Father** and the **Lord** Jesus Christ.*

1 Thessalonians 1:1

*Paul, Silvanus, and Timothy, to the church of the Thessalonians in God the **Father** and the **Lord** Jesus Christ: Grace to you and peace from God our **Father** and the **Lord** Jesus Christ.*

2 Thessalonians 1:2

*Grace to you and peace from God our **Father** and the **Lord** Jesus Christ.*

1 Timothy 1:2

*To Timothy, a true son in the faith: Grace, mercy, and peace from God our **Father** and Jesus Christ our **Lord**.*

2 Timothy 1:2

*To Timothy, a beloved son: Grace, mercy, and peace from God the **Father** and Christ Jesus our **Lord**.*

Titus 1:4

*To Titus, a true son in our common faith: Grace, mercy, and peace from God the **Father** and the **Lord** Jesus Christ our Savior.*

It has not been uncommon throughout scripture for God to talk through man. Many call this the prophetic voice of God. Here are a few scriptural reference points.

Acts 11:16

*Then I remembered the **word** of the **Lord**, how He said, 'John indeed baptized with water, but you shall be baptized with the Holy Spirit.'*

2 Peter 3:2

*That you may be mindful of the **word**s which were spoken before by the holy prophets, and of the commandment of us, the apostles of the **Lord** and Savior.*

2 Chronicles 24:20

*Then the **Spirit** of God came upon Zechariah son of Jehoiada the priest. He stood before the people and **said**, "This is what God says: 'Why do you disobey the LORD's commands? You will not prosper. Because you have forsaken the LORD, he has forsaken you.' "*

Mark 12:36

*For David himself **said** by the Holy **Spirit**: 'The LORD **said** to my Lord," Sit at My right hand, till I make Your enemies Your footstool."'*

Acts 21:11

*When he had come to us, he took Paul's belt, bound his own hands and feet, and **said**, "Thus says the Holy **Spirit**, 'So shall the Jews at Jerusalem bind the man who owns this belt, and deliver him into the hands of the Gentiles.'"*

1 Samuel 12:15

*However, if you do not obey the **voice** of the **LORD**, but rebel against the commandment of the **LORD**, then the hand of the **LORD** will be against you, as it was against your fathers.*

1 Samuel 15:1

*[Saul Spares King Agag] Samuel also said to Saul, "The **LORD** sent me to anoint you king over His people, over Israel. Now therefore, heed the **voice** of the words of the **LORD**.*

Jeremiah 3:12

*Go and proclaim these words toward the north, and say: 'Return, backsliding Israel,' says the **LORD**; 'I will not cause My anger to fall on you. For I am merciful,' says the **LORD**; 'I will not remain angry forever. That you have transgressed against the **LORD** your God, and have scattered your charms to alien deities under every green tree, and you have not obeyed My **voice**,' says the **LORD**.*

Jeremiah 9:13

*And the **LORD** said, "Because they have forsaken My law which I set before them, and have not obeyed My **voice**, nor walked according to it.*

Jeremiah 16:9

*For thus says the **LORD** of hosts, the God of Israel: "Behold, I will cause to cease from this place, before your eyes and in your days, the **voice** of mirth and the **voice** of gladness, the **voice** of the bridegroom and the **voice** of the bride.*

Jeremiah 25:30

*"Therefore prophesy against them all these words, and say to them: 'The **LORD** will roar from on high, and utter His **voice** from His holy habitation; He will roar mightily against His fold. He will give a shout, as those who tread the grapes, against all the inhabitants of the earth.*

Jeremiah 30:5

*"For thus says the **LORD**: 'We have heard a **voice** of trembling, of fear, and not of peace.*

Jeremiah 31:16

*Thus says the **LORD**: "Refrain your **voice** from weeping, And your eyes from tears; For your work shall be rewarded, says the **LORD**, And they shall come back from the land of the enemy.*

Jeremiah 33:11

*The **voice** of joy and the **voice** of gladness, the **voice** of the bridegroom and the **voice** of the bride, the **voice** of those who will say: " Praise the **LORD** of hosts, For the **LORD** is good, For His mercy endures forever" — and of those who will bring the sacrifice of praise into the house of the **LORD**. For I will cause the captives of the land to return as at the first,' says the **LORD**.*

Jeremiah 38:20

*But Jeremiah said, "They shall not deliver you. Please, obey the **voice** of the **LORD** which I speak to you. So it shall be well with you, and your soul shall live.*

Micah 6:1

*[God Pleads with Israel] Hear now what the **LORD**
says:" Arise, plead your case before the mountains,
And let the hills hear your **voice**.*

Nahum 2:13

*"Behold, I am against you," says the **LORD** of hosts,
"I will burn your chariots in smoke, and the sword
shall devour your young lions; I will cut off your prey
from the earth, and the **voice** of your messengers
shall be heard no more."*

Ezekiel 3:24

*Then the **Spirit** entered me and set me on my feet, and
spoke with me and **said** to me: "Go, shut yourself
inside your house.*

Ezekiel 11:5

*Then the **Spirit** of the LORD fell upon me, and **said** to
me, "Speak! 'Thus says the LORD: "Thus you have
said, O house of Israel; for I know the things that
come into your mind.*

Zechariah 4:6

*So he answered and **said** to me: "This is the word
of the LORD to Zerubbabel: 'Not by might nor by
power, but by My **Spirit**,' Says the LORD of hosts.*

Luke 3:22

*And the Holy **Spirit** descended in bodily form like
a dove upon Him, and a voice came from heaven
which **said**, "You are My beloved Son; in You I am
well pleased."*

John 14:26

*But the Helper, the Holy **Spirit**, whom the Father will send in My name, He will teach you all things, and bring to your remembrance all things that I **said** to you.*

Acts 8:29

*Then the **Spirit said** to Philip, "Go near and overtake this chariot."*

Acts 9:17

*And Ananias went his way and entered the house; and laying his hands on him he **said**, "Brother Saul, the Lord Jesus, who appeared to you on the road as you came, has sent me that you may receive your sight and be filled with the Holy **Spirit**."*

Acts 10:19

*While Peter thought about the vision, the **Spirit said** to him, "Behold, three men are seeking you.*

Acts 11:16

*Then I remembered the word of the Lord, how He **said**, 'John indeed baptized with water, but you shall be baptized with the Holy **Spirit**.'*

Acts 13:2

*As they ministered to the Lord and fasted, the Holy **Spirit said**, "Now separate to Me Barnabas and Saul for the work to which I have called them."*

Throughout scripture we are continually taught to not only hear the Voice of God, but to obey His Voice. Obedience is continually described as the key to bringing forth God's purposes. The following scriptures provide prime examples to the necessity of faith and action on the hearer's part.

Hebrews 12:25-29

See that you do not refuse Him who speaks. For if they did not escape who refused Him who spoke on earth, much more shall we not escape if we turn away from Him who speaks from heaven, whose voice then shook the earth; but now He has promised, saying, "Yet once more I shake not only the earth, but also heaven." Now this, "Yet once more," indicates the removal of those things that are being shaken, as of things that are made, that the things which cannot be shaken may remain. Therefore, since we are receiving a kingdom which cannot be shaken, let us have grace, by which we may serve God acceptably with reverence and godly fear. 29 For our God is a consuming fire.

Mark 4:24, 25

Then He said to them, "Take heed what you hear. With the same measure you use, it will be measured to you; and to you who hear, more will be given. For whoever has, to him more will be given; but whoever does not have, even what he has will be taken away from him."

James 1:22

But be doers of the word, and not hearers only, deceiving yourselves.

Hebrews 4:1, 2

Therefore, since a promise remains of entering His rest, let us fear lest any of you seem to have come short of it. For indeed the gospel was preached to us as well as to them; but the word which they heard did not profit them, not being mixed with faith in those who heard it.

Exodus 15:26

*and said, "If you diligently heed the **voice** of the **LORD** your God and do what is right in His sight, give ear to His commandments and keep all His statutes, I will put none of the diseases on you which I have brought on the Egyptians. For I am the **LORD** who heals you."*

Exodus 24:3

*So Moses came and told the people all the words of the **LORD** and all the judgments. And all the people answered with one **voice** and said, "All the words which the **LORD** has said we will do."*

Deuteronomy 13:18

*Because you have listened to the **voice** of the **LORD** your God, to keep all His commandments which I command you today, to do what is right in the eyes of the **LORD** your God.*

Deuteronomy 15:5

*Only if you carefully obey the **voice** of the **LORD** your God, to observe with care all these commandments which I command you today.*

Deuteronomy 26:14

*I have not eaten any of it when in mourning, nor have I removed any of it for an unclean use, nor given any of it for the dead. I have obeyed the **voice** of the **LORD** my God, and have done according to all that You have commanded me.*

Deuteronomy 26:17

*Today you have proclaimed the **LORD** to be your God, and that you will walk in His ways and keep His statutes, His commandments, and His judgments, and that you will obey His **voice**.*

Deuteronomy 27:10

*Therefore you shall obey the **voice** of the **LORD** your God, and observe His commandments and His statutes which I command you today."*

Deuteronomy 28:1

*[Blessings on Obedience] "Now it shall come to pass, if you diligently obey the **voice** of the **LORD** your God, to observe carefully all His commandments which I command you today, that the **LORD** your God will set you high above all nations of the earth.*

Deuteronomy 28:2

*And all these blessings shall come upon you and overtake you, because you obey the **voice** of the **LORD** your God.*

Deuteronomy 28:15

*[Curses on Disobedience] "But it shall come to pass, if you do not obey the **voice** of the **LORD** your God, to observe carefully all His commandments and His*

statutes which I command you today, that all these curses will come upon you and overtake you.

Deuteronomy 28:45

*"Moreover all these curses shall come upon you and pursue and overtake you, until you are destroyed, because you did not obey the **voice** of the **LORD** your God, to keep His commandments and His statutes which He commanded you.*

Deuteronomy 28:62

*You shall be left few in number, whereas you were as the stars of heaven in multitude, because you would not obey the **voice** of the **LORD** your God.*

Deuteronomy 30:2

*And you return to the **LORD** your God and obey His **voice**, according to all that I command you today, you and your children, with all your heart and with all your soul.*

Deuteronomy 30:8

*And you will again obey the **voice** of the **LORD** and do all His commandments which I command you today.*

Deuteronomy 30:10

*If you obey the **voice** of the **LORD** your God, to keep His commandments and His statutes which are written in this Book of the Law, and if you turn to the **LORD** your God with all your heart and with all your soul.*

Deuteronomy 30:20

That you may love the LORD your God, that you may obey His voice, and that you may cling to Him, for He is your life and the length of your days; and that you may dwell in the land which the LORD swore to your fathers, to Abraham, Isaac, and Jacob, to give them."

Joshua 5:6

For the children of Israel walked forty years in the wilderness, till all the people who were men of war, who came out of Egypt, were consumed, because they did not obey the voice of the LORD—to whom the LORD swore that He would not show them the land which the LORD had sworn to their fathers that He would give us, "a land flowing with milk and honey".

Joshua 22:2

And said to them: "You have kept all that Moses the servant of the LORD commanded you, and have obeyed my voice in all that I commanded you.

Joshua 24:24

And the people said to Joshua, "The LORD our God we will serve, and His voice we will obey!"

Judges 2:20

Then the anger of the LORD was hot against Israel; and He said, "Because this nation has transgressed My covenant which I commanded their fathers, and has not heeded My voice.

Judges 6:10

*Also I said to you, "I am the **LORD** your God; do not fear the gods of the Amorites, in whose land you dwell." But you have not obeyed My **voice**.*

1 Samuel 12:15

*However, if you do not obey the **voice** of the **LORD**, but rebel against the commandment of the **LORD**, then the hand of the **LORD** will be against you, as it was against your fathers.*

1 Samuel 15:1

*[Saul Spares King Agag] Samuel also said to Saul, "The **LORD** sent me to anoint you king over His people, over Israel. Now therefore, heed the **voice** of the words of the **LORD**.*

1 Samuel 15:19

*Why then did you not obey the **voice** of the **LORD**? Why did you swoop down on the spoil, and do evil in the sight of the **LORD**?"*

1 Samuel 15:20

*And Saul said to Samuel, "But I have obeyed the **voice** of the **LORD**, and gone on the mission on which the **LORD** sent me, and brought back Agag king of Amalek; I have utterly destroyed the Amalekites.*

1 Samuel 15:22

*So Samuel said: "Has the **LORD** as great delight in burnt offerings and sacrifices, As in obeying the **voice** of the **LORD**? Behold, to obey is better than sacrifice, And to heed than the fat of rams.*

1 Samuel 28:18

*Because you did not obey the **voice** of the **LORD** nor execute His fierce wrath upon Amalek, therefore the **LORD** has done this thing to you this day.*

1 Kings 20:36

*Then he said to him, "Because you have not obeyed the **voice** of the **LORD**, surely, as soon as you depart from me, a lion shall kill you." And as soon as he left him, a lion found him and killed him.*

2 Kings 18:12

*Because they did not obey the **voice** of the **LORD** their God, but transgressed His covenant and all that Moses the servant of the **LORD** had commanded; and they would neither hear nor do them.*

Jeremiah 3:25

*We lie down in our shame, And our reproach covers us. For we have sinned against the **LORD** our God, We and our fathers, From our youth even to this day, And have not obeyed the **voice** of the **LORD** our God."*

Jeremiah 7:28

*[Judgment on Obscene Religion] "So you shall say to them, 'This is a nation that does not obey the **voice** of the **LORD** their God nor receive correction. Truth has perished and has been cut off from their mouth.*

Jeremiah 38:20

*But Jeremiah said, "They shall not deliver you. Please, obey the **voice** of the **LORD** which I speak to you. So it shall be well with you, and your soul shall live.*

Jeremiah 40:3

*Now the **LORD** has brought it, and has done just as He said. Because you people have sinned against the **LORD**, and not obeyed His **voice**, therefore this thing has come upon you.*

Jeremiah 42:6

*Whether it is pleasing or displeasing, we will obey the **voice** of the **LORD** our God to whom we send you, that it may be well with us when we obey the **voice** of the **LORD** our God."*

Jeremiah 42:13

*"But if you say, 'We will not dwell in this land,' disobeying the **voice** of the **LORD** your God,*

Jeremiah 42:21

*And I have this day declared it to you, but you have not obeyed the **voice** of the **LORD** your God, or anything which He has sent you by me.*

Jeremiah 43:4

*So Johanan the son of Kareah, all the captains of the forces, and all the people would not obey the **voice** of the **LORD**, to remain in the land of Judah.*

Jeremiah 43:7

*So they went to the land of Egypt, for they did not obey the **voice** of the **LORD**. And they went as far as Tahpanhes.*

Jeremiah 44:23

*Because you have burned incense and because you have sinned against the **LORD**, and have not obeyed the **voice** of the **LORD** or walked in His law, in His* *statutes or in His testimonies, therefore this calamity has happened to you, as at this day."*

Daniel 9:10

*We have not obeyed the **voice** of the **LORD** our God, to walk in His laws, which He set before us by His servants the prophets.*

Daniel 9:14

*Therefore the **LORD** has kept the disaster in mind, and brought it upon us; for the **LORD** our God is righteous in all the works which He does, though we have not obeyed His **voice**.*

Breinigsville, PA USA
22 August 2009
222761BV00002B/1/P

9 781606 477540